THE
FRANCISCANS
IN ENGLAND

by

JOHN R. H. MOORMAN
Bishop of Ripon

MOWBRAYS
LONDON & OXFORD

BOOKS BY THE SAME AUTHOR

Sources for the Life of St Francis
Church Life in England in the Thirteenth Century
A New Fioretti
B. K. Cunningham, a Memoir
St Francis of Assisi
The Grey Friars in Cambridge
A History of the Church in England
The Curate of Souls
The Path to Glory
Vatican Observed
A History of the Franciscan Order

Copyright © 1974 J.R.H. Moorman

*Set in IBM 11/12 Press Roman by Hope Services, Wantage
and printed and bound by Redwood Burn Limited,
Trowbridge & Esher.*

ISBN 0 264 66186 9 (paperback)
ISBN 0 264 66234 2 (hardback)

*First published 1974 by A.R. Mowbray & Co Ltd
The Alden Press, Osney Mead, Oxford, OX2 OEG*

CONTENTS

FOREWORD

The most significant thing about this book is that it was written by a Bishop of the Church of England. A few years ago it would have seemed strange; but to-day, such is the fellow feeling among Christians, Anglicans regard a saint as belonging to them just as much as to the Church which decreed his canonisation. The 'them' and 'us' mentality is disappearing. Despite the centuries of anti-papalism we have actually seen a modern pope become a hero in every Christian home. It is true that Pope John was unique among popes. It is none the less true that St. Francis is unique among saints. Bishop Moorman sums it up by calling St. Francis a human saint and gives this as the reason for his popularity among Anglicans.

The Bishop makes the important point that Franciscans are not all cloistered monks. They are not necessarily priests or nuns. There are, of course, Friars and Poor Clares but within the worldwide Franciscan family there are thousands in what is called the Third Order. These tertiaries are mostly lay people seeking to model their lives on the teaching and example of Francis of Assisi. In past centuries they used to live in communities but the Franciscan spirit can be perfectly well observed by husbands and wives and unmarried men and women leading normal working lives. It is opportune to be reminded by this book that we can become Franciscans without forsaking home and family.

Some readers will be surprised to learn that the Franciscan Order is well established in the Anglican communion. It may even surprise some to discover that an Anglican Bishop is perhaps the best known Franciscan scholar in the English-speaking world. It is fitting that the year 1974, seven and a half centuries after the coming of the Franciscans to England, should be marked by a tribute from the Bishop's pen. As an ecclesiastical historian he is acknowledged to be a leading authority on Franciscan lore. Happily for us he has written this account of the Franciscans in England not for scholars but for all who admire St. Francis.

The Poor Man of Assisi is indeed a human saint but he is much more. He is the character above all others in religious history who saw God in everything. Because of his passionate love of the Creator he worshipped Him in the whole of creation. The birds and the beasts were his brothers and sisters. He loved God above all things and saw God in the least of his creatures. At a time when greed is so obviously destroying the world or, as we fashionably say, polluting the environment, this may be the ideal moment to recall the gentle Francis who taught men and women the beauty of poverty accepted for the love of God.

March 1974   + JOHN CARD. HEENAN
                                ARCHBISHOP OF WESTMINSTER

1

THE FRANCISCANS

On Tuesday, 10th September, 1224, a ship put in at
Dover Harbour having come from some port in northern
France. As the passengers disembarked there was seen to
be among them, a little group of nine men all scantily
clad in old, patched garments and with nothing on their
feet. They had no luggage as they had all taken a vow to
have no possessions of any kind; but this did not seem to
worry them in the least. As soon as they had alighted
from the ship they set off in the direction of Canterbury.

This little group of nine men, of various ages and
nationalities, were all members of the religious order
which had emerged in Italy some fifteen years ago as the
result of the genius, inspiration and courage of a man
known as Francis of Assisi. Those who followed him were
officially called 'Friars Minor' but they were also known
as Greyfriars or as Franciscans.

Francesco Bernardone, whom we now know as Saint
Francis of Assisi, was born in the little Italian town of
Assisi about the year 1182, the son of a prosperous
merchant who travelled about the cities of Italy and
France buying and selling cloth. Francis received his
education in Assisi, and grew up to be a high-spirited
young man, much concerned with the pursuit of pleasure
but known to be imaginative and unconventional. He
quickly became a natural leader among other young men
of the town who found him attractive and enterprising.
But, in addition to his jollifications, he was known also to
have a remarkable interest in the poor, of which any
Italian city in those days was full.

Like most of his contemporaries, Francis aspired to a life of enterprise and glory, hoping thus to win the approval of his friends and to bring honour to his family. He joined the young men of Assisi in a skirmish with their old rivals, the people of Perugia, and spent a year as a prisoner of war. He then set off on a military expedition to southern Italy to fight for the Church against its enemies. But these knightly hopes soon faded as Francis learnt that this was not the sort of life which he was intended to live. From now onwards he began to take more interest in the poor, the lepers, the beggars, the people who were condemned to a life of hardship and misery. It would, of course, have been quite easy for Francis to have joined his father in the textile business and to have used the money which he made in doing good works among the under-privileged. But Francis did not see his life in this way. Gradually he came to realise that if he was to help the poor it must be by becoming one of them, by accepting and sharing their privations, by giving up all comfort and all security.

Together with this desire to share in the sufferings of the poor went a strong conviction that God was calling him to be a new apostle, to go from place to place telling people about God and to show them how to live in obedience to the teaching of Christ. Francis saw himself as an evangelist, but not like others working in the Lord's Vineyard, the parochial clergy of the members of the religious orders. Francis believed that people would listen to him more readily if they saw that he was modelling his life on that of Christ and his apostles.

The stages whereby Francis cut himself adrift from the life in which he had been brought up can be read in any standard life of the Saint. The process ended in the little tumble-down church of the Portiuncula outside Assisi on

24th February, 1206, when he heard the words of Christ when he sent out his apostles: 'Preach saying the Kingdom of Heaven is at hand. Heal the sick; cleanse the lepers; raise the dead; cast out devils. Freely you have received; freely give. Provide neither gold nor silver nor brass in your purses, nor scrip for your journey; neither two coats, neither shoes nor yet staves, for the workman is worthy of his meat.' To Francis this seemed a personal message. Once again Christ needed his messengers to go out in his name and preach his gospel. Francis was overjoyed to think that he was to be one of them and was more than ready to accept the conditions which Christ laid down.

So Francis went out of that little church determined to take quite literally the words of Christ and to follow them out at whatever the cost. He was to go about telling people about God and about his kingdom. He was to tell them about Jesus and what he had said to the people of his generation. He was to show them that no command of Christ was impossible for he was to obey with the utmost strictness every order which Christ had given.

He was, then, to ask nothing for himself, to have no possessions of any kind and to depend entirely on the mercy of God and the generosity and goodwill of his fellow-men. He was to live among the poorest of the poor, regardless of his own needs, comforts or health, even if this meant living and eating with lepers with all the danger and horror which this involved. He was often cold and hungry. He was sometimes laughed at and insulted. Occasionally he was assaulted. For twenty years he endured this hard life, and he died at the age of forty-four, blind and in great pain.

For a year or two Francis was a solitary seeker after perfection. He had few friends, but many critics. But he was being watched. How long, people were asking, can this rather fastidious young man endure this kind of life? Some thought that he would die of starvation or exposure some cold night in the Umbrian mountains. Others thought that he would undoubtedly catch leprosy or some other terrible disease and die a lingering death in some hovel. Few thought that he would attract others to a life of such hardship and insecurity.

But there were others who were both interested and impressed. A wealthy young man with such good prospects must, they said, have very strong convictions before taking up this sort of life. Was it possible that he was doing something which would bring new vigour and credibility to the Church? Most people thought he was mad; but there were one or two who began to think that he was a saint and a prophet.

Among these was another wealthy man in Assisi called Bernard of Quintavalle, older than Francis and a man of considerable standing in the city. He was one of those who was watching ... and thinking ... and asking himself some awkward questions. So one night Bernard invited Francis to his house and next morning he decided to give away all his possessions and join Francis in his life of poverty and service. Soon after that others came along— a priest, a labourer, a poet, other young men living in Assisi. Thus a little fraternity was built up, a little group of men of different ages and backgrounds, who were prepared to give up all that they had and embark upon a life of absolute poverty and simplicity, of total commitment and total trust, in response to the teaching of Christ as interpreted by their leader, Francis.

When Francis had accepted his marching-orders from Christ in the little church of the Portiuncula he had probably no idea that other men might hear the same message and make the same decisions. For a year or two he was certainly alone in his task. But with the coming of these other men everything took on a new aspect. The solitary evangelist, content to live with the lepers, was now the acknowledged leader of a community with all the responsibilities which that entailed. Francis was delighted. He had visions now of his work being extended all over Europe and perhaps further afield. Instead of one man preaching and living the Gospel it looked now as if there were going to be a great many of them, with what results no one could foresee.

When the little brotherhood had attracted twelve re-cruits Francis decided that the time had come to make some plans for their future. There were other bands of itinerant evangelists wandering about Europe, some very critical of the Church and demanding liberty and independence. Francis had no wish to do that. His literal obedience to Christ meant also literal obedience to the Church. Christ could not possibly want his new servants to be disloyal to the Church which they were to honour and support. Francis was, therefore, shrewd enough to see that if the ambitions and hopes of his brotherhood were to be ful-filled they would need to have some authority, some recognition, as otherwise they would almost certainly be prevented from going ahead.

So, in 1209, the twelve Poor Men of Assisi decided to go to Rome to see the pope and to try to persuade him to treat them seriously as devoted servants of the Church and to give them his blessing. It is known that Francis wrote down some primitive form of Rule at this stage, setting out what their intentions were and based largely on quotations from the words of Christ. Neither this Rule, nor the bedraggled appearance of the little band who had been sleeping rough for some time, were likely to impress the Holy Father; but Innocent III was himself a wise and

holy man who, after some misgivings, began to see the
sincerity and courage of these men and gave them authority to preach the gospel of repentance. Six years later,
when the Lateran Council tried to put an end to new
religious orders, Innocent saw to it that the followers of
Francis were allowed to continue.

From now onwards things began to happen fairly
quickly. The little brotherhood of twelve poor men, under
the personal leadership of Francis, rapidly grew into an
order of considerable size, and the 'friars minor' came
to be a familiar sight as they travelled about Italy. Francis
normally sent them out in pairs in accordance with
apostolic practice. They worked on the land or used their
particular skills in order to earn their keep. At the end of
the day they asked for food and shelter but were strictly
forbidden to accept money, a commodity which Francis
always regarded as untouchable. If their employer treated
them decently they would get the necessities of life; but
if he refused to give them anything, or if they failed to
get work, they begged their food from door to door and
slept in churches and barns. In addition to their manual
labour they preached to any who would listen to them.
Those whom they attracted to their sermons varied very
greatly—sometimes just a few children or a handful of
peasants, sometimes quite large congregations in the
churches. Francis himself preached fairly often in the
cathedral church in Assisi.

It was a hard, rough life, but one which each of them
had deliberately chosen, making poverty an ideal to be
worked for. St. Francis, in his romantic way, used to
talk about 'Lady Poverty' as the bride whom he wished
to woo and make his own. But poverty was not their
only ideal. Brother Leo tells us that the four things which
the friars prized above all else were Poverty, Humility,

Simplicity and Prayer.

We must, therefore, imagine these men wandering from village to village and from town to town, preaching, working, serving the poor, setting an example of Christian life and obedience quite different from the sort of thing which was practised by clergy and laity alike. At a time when some of the parish priests were disillusioned, ignorant and incompetent, when those in the higher ranks of the clergy were often rich and worldly, and when the monks were busy looking after their vast estates and their commodious monasteries, there was something compelling and arresting about these followers of St. Francis—so cheerful, so attractive, so courageous as they went their way, talking about God and bringing new hope and joy into the lives of men and women everywhere.

It is not surprising that the Order of Friars Minor grew rapidly; but the rate and extent of this growth produced a number of problems. At first no one could become a member of the community unless Francis was satisfied that he came with the right motives and that he would, unhesitatingly, accept the way of life which they had chosen. Francis was very strict in his judgements, and many young men who expressed a wish to join the Order were turned away. But as the Order spread further afield it became impossible for every postulant to be interviewed by St. Francis himself. Individual friars thus, inevitably, assumed that they had the right to admit men on their own initiative. It was not long, therefore, before men became friars without ever having seen St. Francis, perhaps in some country which the saint had never visited.

Francis regarded the world as his parish and went wherever the Spirit directed him. In 1212 he decided to go off to the East in the hopes of putting an end to the Crusades and perhaps himself being martyred for the cause; but he got no farther than the eastern shores of the Adriatic. In 1213 he tried to reach the Moslem world through the western approaches, but he got held up by sickness in Spain. Later on he managed to get to Egypt and made his way into the tent of the Sultan himself in the hopes of converting him to the Christian faith, though, not unnaturally, without success. There was, therefore, a great deal of movement going on, the friars going wherever they liked with little or no planning or organisation.

In order to keep in touch with one another it became their practice to meet once a year at the Portiuncula where Francis had received his final orders. Here at Pentecost the friars assembled from all over Europe. There were no buildings except the little chapel, so they slept in the open air or built little huts out of the branches of trees. Then for several days they would pray together, discuss their work and lay their plans for the future. Clearly, if the work was to prosper, there must be some allocation of duties and some organisation. Up till now there was nothing much in the way of a Rule to which friars could vow obedience. The flimsy collection of texts which Francis had presented to Innocent III in 1209 was now out of date and had to be replaced first by the Rule of 1221, which never had any official recognition, and then by the shorter, and slightly less demanding Rule of 1223 which received papal sanction. This meant that anyone wishing to join the Order would at least have some idea as to what he was letting himself in for.

Meanwhile the Order was beginning to plan out its work, and, in 1217, it decided to set up a number of 'provinces', each under the jurisdiction of a 'provincial minister' who would exercise some authority over the friars and see that the simple little Rule was observed. In this year six provinces were set up for Italy, two for

France, and one each for Germany, Spain and the Holy Land. With the organisation of the Order came also some changes in the friar's way of life. Up till now they had been homeless wanderers, content to go wherever they thought they were needed and asking nothing for themselves. But they now found it convenient to have lodgings of some kind in various places. Some of these were old, disused monasteries or churches which they were allowed to use. In other places small houses were provided by the citizens who liked to have a more or less permanent settlement to which the friars could go. But the itinerant, evangelistic ideal still held good and many friars were opposed to the use of permanent houses. If Francis came upon a building which he thought too good he ordered the friars to abandon it; and once he climbed on the roof of a building and started to demolish it with his own hands. He was not going to allow the Lady Poverty to be insulted.

The problem of maintaining a high ideal of poverty and simplicity and yet be an organised, religious Order with a Rule and with its own officials was one which caused Francis a lot of worry and distress in the latter years of his life. If it is true, that at the Chapter of the Mats, which was held about 1220, there were 5,000 friars present, it gives some idea both of the progress of the Order and of the problems which now had to be faced. Whereas in its origins the Order had been almost entirely a lay movement, it now contained a large number of priests who had certain vows to perform which required the use of books, altars and other equipment. Others were scholars who wished to contribute their intellectual ability to the teaching and evangelistic work of the Order but who could not do this without books and other amenities.

Meanwhile the Church authorities saw in this movement something which could be of immense value to them so long as they had some say in its development. Francis, in spite of his loyalty and obedience, was inclined to resist this as he thought it would inevitably reduce the standard of poverty and of dependence upon God which he regarded as the basis of his whole experimeent in Christian living. He did not want property, or privilege, or security for his followers. He wanted them just to serve God and man in humble self-sacrifice and penury. So there was tension; and there were moments when Francis was very unhappy. 'Who are those' he once cried, 'who snatch my Order and my brethern out of my hands?'. But by this time things had gone too far. The idyllic life of those early days had largely disappeared. Francis, though unwillingly, was now the head of a big religious Order which was making its mark all over the world.

By 1219, if not before, the friars had reached Paris and had established a house big enough to contain thirty men. In the same year they had sent an expedition into Germany but this came to grief as none of the friars seems to have had any knowledge of the German language. As a result, they were mistaken for heretics and came in for a good deal of opposition and assault when they were unable to explain their intentions. In the following year, however, another party set out with a German friar called Caesar of Speyer as their leader, and this time all went well.

Then, in 1223 or 1224, it was decided to send an expedition to England. Already one or two Englishmen had joined the order, including Brother William who became a personal friend of St. Francis and lies buried close to the saint in the great basilica in Assisi. Others had encountered the movement somewhere in Europe, perhaps in France or Germany. So when the party destined for England was made up, the friars, remembering what had happened in Germany, included three Englishmen in the party.

The leader of the group was Agnellus of Pisa, a deacon, now aged about thirty. He had probably joined the Order as a result of hearing St. Francis preach in Pisa about 1211. Six years later he had gone to France where he had done such good work that he was made *custos* of Paris, an office which gave him some authority over the other houses in the neighbourhood. His right-hand man was an Englishman called Richard of Ingworth, a good deal older than Agnellus and a priest. Richard seems to have thought out a plan for their work in England and helped Agnellus to prepare for work in a country of strange language. The other two Englishmen were Richard of Devon and William of Esseby, who were both young.

The other five friars in the party were all foreigners and all laymen—Henry of Treviso from Lombardy, Laurence of Beauvais, William of Florence, Melioratus and James, who was only a novice.

This was the little party which landed at Dover in 1224 to promote the work which Francis had begun.

2

THE COMING OF
THE FRIARS TO ENGLAND

It was probably evening when the friars landed at Dover
having come from some port on the north coast of
France, their fares paid for them by the Benedictine
monks of Fécamp. The party had most likely been assembled in Paris, where Agnellus was living, and had made its
way down the valley of the Seine to Fécamp where they
had obviously won the respect and co-operation of the
monks.

They did not intend to make any settlement in Dover,
their first object being to get as far as Canterbury, sixteen
miles away. But they were obliged to spend their first
night somewhere near Dover, and they approached what
looked like a promising place at which to beg for food
and shelter. This was a large house on the outskirts of the
town; but when the owner saw this shabby little group of
men in their patched habits and bare feet he not unnaturally came to the conclusion that they were spies
and robbers and immediately locked them up. On the
following morning he had them led before the justices
and accused them of being thieves. But as soon as he had
done this one of the friars, in a jovial spirit, took off the
cord which he wore round his waist and said: 'if you
think we are those sort of people here is a rope to hang
us with.' The justices of the peace were so impressed by
this that they immediately let them go.

So they walked on to Canterbury where they sought
hospitality with the monks of Christ Church, the cathedral monastery. It is possible that they brought a letter

of commendation from the monks of Fécamp; but whether they had this or not, they were taken in and housed for two days during which they tried to find somewhere to live as they wanted to establish a small community in the city as soon as possible.

Five of the friars stayed in Canterbury to see what could be done while the other four—Richard of Ingworth, Richard of Devon, Henry of Treviso and Melioratus—set out for London. Agnellus and the three who remained with him soon found a friend in the warden of the Priests' Hospice who took them under his care. For a time they were housed in a small room at the back of a school until the warden, Alexander of Gloucester, could find something better for them. The conditions were obviously very cramped, and we are told that, when the boys had gone home, the friars used to go into the schoolroom and make up the fire. They then collected the dregs of beer which the boys had left behind, added some water to them, heated them up on the fire and then drank the brew while each contributed some word of edification.

This did not last very long as the warden gave them part of the garden of the Hospice and built them a small chapel. Nothing is said of living accommodation, but they probably managed to rig up some huts in which they could live. As the friars were not allowed by their Rule to own any property, the land and the buildings were vested in the city authorities. And here, in these very simple quarters, the Greyfriars of Canterbury lived for nearly fifty years, until, in 1267 a citizen called John Digges acquired some land on the other side of the river Stour so that more convenient buildings could be erected. All that remains of the new friary is a small building built over the stream which divided their original site from where they eventually settled.

There is no doubt that the little community soon began to grow. The people of Canterbury were obviously pleased to have them and appreciated and admired what they were doing and their obvious courage and sincerity. It is unlikely that the archbishop, Stephen Langton, saw anything of them in these early days, but his brother, Simon, who was Archdeacon of Canterbury befriended them, together with Lord Henry of Sandwich and that remarkable lady called Loretta, Countess of Leicester, who lived as a recluse just outside the city. But though the archbishop may not have been present to welcome them into his see city he very quickly became interested in them; and when the first novice, Solomon, was presented to him for ordination as an acolyte he referred to him as Brother Solomon 'of the Order of the Apostles', which delighted the friars who regarded it as recognition of their obedience to the commands of Christ. The archbishop was himself much impressed by the fact that Brother Solomon, when he had been regaled at the archbishop's table, went off barefoot into the snow to walk the 56 miles from London to Canterbury.

We do not know how quickly the Canterbury community grew, though, by 1289, there were sixty friars in the house. This was perhaps exceptional, and we should probably be wise to think of the number of friars being normally between thirty-five and forty. But numbers varied from time to time. Friaries were very different from monasteries which had more or less static communities of men who remained in one place all their lives. Friars were essentially mobile, moving from house to house, which would account for considerable variation. Of the five original members of the community, Agnellus soon went off to London and William of Esseby, though only a young man, was put in charge of the house at

14

Oxford, Laurence of Beauvais was a personal friend of St. Francis and went back to Italy to spend some time with him before his death in 1226. It is said that Francis gave Laurence his own habit and a special blessing before he died. William of Florence returned to France; but of James nothing is known.

While Agnellus and his four companions were settling in at Canterbury, Richard of Ingworth led the other three to London. Here they were kindly welcomed by the Dominican friars who gave them hospitality for fifteen days while they looked for somewhere to live. Before long they found a house in Cornhill where they spent some months, making the house look something like a religious community by building little cells, plugging the cracks between the timber with dried grass. They had no chapel at first, so they said their offices in the house and went to Mass in a local church. After Richard of Ingworth went off to Oxford in October they had no priest until Philip of London joined them later on. Others who joined the community in these early days were William of London, a young scholar, Jocelin of Cornhill, a youth of noble birth, and a lad of eighteen called John who was in minor orders.

Whether all of these were actually received into the London house is not certain, but there is no doubt that the community there grew fairly rapidly for, by the summer of 1225, the house in Cornhill had become much too small for them and something larger had to be sought. At this point a wealthy merchant called John Iwyn bought for their use a plot of ground in Stinking Lane, near New-gate. This, which was close to the Shambles, was obviously not a very salubrious place, as the name implies. But, as was the custom in the Middle Ages when people of all classes lived close together, a number of rich men seem to have had their homes in the same area. On this plot of ground a house was built more adapted to the life of a religious community. The King, Henry III, helped by sending some timber from Windsor forest and, some years later he sent 700 ells of cloth, some white and some grey to help clothe the Dominicans and Franciscans in London, together with 100 pairs of shoes for the Dominicans since the followers of St. Francis preferred to go barefoot. The buildings which they erected on this site were at first very simple and unpretentious, and no attempt was made to enclose the area as was normally done for a religious house. When William of Nottingham, the Provincial Minister, was criticised by some people for not enclosing the London house he said: 'I didn't join the friars in order to build walls'; and when he saw what he regarded as some unnecessary ornament to the church and cloister he ordered it to be removed.

While this was going on the two English friars, Richard of Ingworth and Richard of Devon, had left London and gone to Oxford. It was essential, if the Order was to make any mark in the country, that new members should be found as quickly as possible. Canterbury was an important ecclesiastical centre where young men might be expected to assemble. London was the largest city in the country. Oxford was full of students some of whom might make very good friars if they could be attracted into the Order. So to Oxford they went, and, the two friars were given immediate hospitality by the Dominicans with whom they stayed for eight days. But they were soon given a house by Robert the Mercer in which they lived until the summer of 1225. During these months the number of friars increased rapidly as 'many honest bachelors and many eminent men' now joined the Order. This meant that a larger house was necessary and a man called Richard the

Miller came to their rescue with a house with a garden attached to it. This was eventually presented to the city to be used by the friars.

Strict rules of poverty and simplicity were observed. The Rule said that friars must not accept money, and when the Archdeacon of Northampton sent a bag of money one of the friars, Adam Marsh, refused to accept it. The messenger, annoyed at having made a fruitless journey, threw it down on the ground. Adam then had it returned to the archdeacon with the request that he would use it for some other purpose. In this sort of way the friars showed people that they were in earnest in observing the wishes of their founder. They were adamant, too, about not wearing shoes in spite of the fact that the Rule was drawn up by people living in a warmer climate than England. A contemporary chronicler tells us of two friars returning from a Chapter meeting at Oxford at Christmastime singing hymns as they 'picked their way along the rugged path over the frozen mud and hard snow, while the blood lay in the track of their naked feet without being conscious of it.' Yet in spite of the hardships they remained a remarkably cheerful crowd. One of the younger friars at Oxford was so given to laughter that he was ordered to be beaten every time he laughed in choir or at table. But even this did not control him, though he was known to have received as many as eleven beatings in one day. In the end he was sobered by a terrifying dream which warned him of the dangers ahead.

There is no doubt that the Oxford friary quickly became a lively and exciting place. In 1233 there were forty friars there, many of them, no doubt, attending the lectures which the friars had arranged in the new school which was now being built for them in which the most prominent theologian in Oxford, Robert Grosseteste, was now lecturing.

17

As soon as Richard of Ingworth and his young companion, Richard of Devon, had got the Oxford house established they set off again on their travels, this time to Northampton. Here they stayed for a short time in a hospital—possibly among lepers and paupers—until they could get a house to live in. This was soon provided for them by Sir Robert Gobion whose son, John, became a friar.

From this point onwards it is difficult to determine the precise order in which the next few houses were founded; but, after the successes at Oxford, it was natural for the friars to consider the sister university town of Cambridge. It is not certain when the friars first arrived in Cambridge, but it was probably in 1225. Here they were lodged in a building known as 'the house of Benjamin the Jew' in the centre of the town. It had for a time been used partly as a dwelling-house and partly as a synagogue, and its position can be determined from the fact that when the foundations of the present Guildhall were being dug in 1782 the remains of some tombstones with Hebrew inscriptions were found. By the time the friars arrived, part of the house was empty while the other part had been turned into the town jail. It was in this house that the friars lived for over forty years until they built their own friary on land where Sidney Sussex College now stands.

The house of Benjamin the Jew was obviously not a very comfortable place in which to live. There was only one entrance for prisoners, jailers and friars. Some of the prisoners may have been a nuisance. Drunks and disorderlies locked up for the night may well have disturbed the friars' devotions or prevented them from getting any sleep. There was at first no chapel, though, after a time, the friars got hold of a piece of land adjoining the house and built themselves a small chapel, so small and simple that a single carpenter, in one day, made and put up fifteen pairs of rafters for the roof. But all this was, of course, very much in accordance with Francis' wishes that, if the friars were to have any buildings at all, they should be poor and insignificant.

The Cambridge community was at first very small. Eccleston says that there were only three clerks—William of Esseby, whom we last heard of in Canterbury, Hugh de Bugeton, and a lame novice called Elias. But there were also some lay brothers including Thomas of Spain who was probably one of the 'Knights' who joined the Order in London. Though small the community was, however, renowned for its devotion and for its poverty. Inspite of intermittent noises from the jail we are told that the friars 'sang the offices devoutly with notation', and, in spite of living in a cold, damp climate, they refused to allow themselves the use of cloaks.

The friars had come to Cambridge in order to get recruits; but when the Oxford community set up a school, the Cambridge friars decided to do the same. Since there was as yet no faculty of theology at Cambridge the friars had to find their own lecturers and appointed Vincent of Coventry to do this. Vincent, who had joined the Order in 1225 was known to be a good scholar. He probably began his lectures at Cambridge about five years later.

During these five years (1225–1230) we know that at least twelve more Franciscan houses were founded—in the cathedral cities of Norwich, Worcester, Hereford, Salisbury, York and Lincoln; in the ports of Bristol and Lynn, and in the important towns of Gloucester, Nottingham, Leicester and Stamford. This shows that the friars were making for the places where they would find most to do—towns where there were a lot of poor people to minister to, and where they could hope to get good opportunities for preaching the Gospel. After 1230 the foundation of houses continued, so that, by the year 1255, thirty-one years after their arrival in England, there were forty-nine houses in the country containing 1,242 friars. By this time communities had been formed in five more cathedral cities—Chichester, Carlisle, Winchester, Lichfield and Exeter.

There is no doubt that life was hard for the friars during the first fifty years until the great new building programmes came about. They were mostly living in ordinary houses or in make-shift huts. In getting themselves started they had depended largely on lay help, sometimes given by wealthy benefactors but more often by the local citizens. Occasionally, as at Salisbury, it was the bishop who helped to find them somewhere to live. On at least one occasion it was a local monastery who came to their aid, as at Reading where the monks gave them land on which to build. The ordinary people welcomed them because they realised that the friars had come to work among them. They liked to see the friars going in and out among the sick and the poor. They liked to listen to them preaching, not only when they were expounding the Scriptures but also when they told them stories or spoke of their experiences in foreign parts. They admired their sincerity and austerity when they saw them walking barefoot through the snow or huddled together in draughty little sheds. Here was a new kind of ministry, something which they could understand and respect.

Of course, there was some opposition. Some of the local clergy were naturally suspicious of men who started working in their parishes. Some of them may well have been jealous of freelance preachers who enticed their congregations away on Sunday mornings by their eloquence and wit. Some criticised the friars for hearing confessions, especially as Canon Law made it quite clear that it was the privilege of the parish priest to do this. The setting up of a Franciscan community in a town might well cause considerable consternation and perhaps some opposition.

The monks and canons of the older established religious Orders were also inclined to be hostile. Perhaps they felt that the friars, by living so simply and austerely, were drawing attention to the luxury and ease which existed in many of the monasteries. Perhaps they were afraid that the friars would stir up discontent among their poorer tenants in the cities. Perhaps they felt that the supply of novices would dry up as so many young men seemed to want to join one of the new Orders. Whatever their reasons, there is no doubt that the monks did not much like the friars; and many of them would have nodded their heads in approval if they had come across the words of one of their chroniclers who, writing of the year 1224, said: 'In that same year, O Misery, O more than Misery, O Cruel Scourge, the Friars Minor came to England'.

Once the friars got established the monks could do very little to interfere with their work; but, on more than one occasion, an existing religious house did its utmost to prevent the friars from setting up an establishment anywhere near them. The most striking example of this was at Bury St. Edmunds, where there was a large and powerful Benedictine abbey which contained about eighty monks with a large following of chaplains, servants and others to look after them. The town of Bury St. Edmunds had grown up around the abbey which owned most of the houses and land. The Franciscans made their first attempt to settle here in 1233, but it came to nothing. Over twenty years later, in 1257, they made a second

21

attempt, fortified with a faculty from the pope, Alexander IV. Knowing that there might be opposition they arrived under cover of darkness, carrying a portable altar, and settled in a farm-house at the northern end of the town. Hearing of this, the monks were extremely indignant, and sent men to drive them out. The friars refused to move and appealed to the pope who ordered the monks to leave them alone. This the monks refused to do and made another attempt to get rid of them. So the friars then appealed to the King, and, with his support, managed to maintain a precarious foothold for a few years. But, in 1261, the new pope, Urban IV, took up the monks' cause, and the friars were obliged to leave the town and settle at Babwell a few miles away. A somewhat similar quarrel arose between the friars of Scarborough and the Cistercians.

But, by and large, the friars settled down quickly and peacefully, and this was undoubtedly due to the wisdom and tact of the first few leaders or Provincial Ministers. Agnellus of Pisa was the first of these. His policy was to maintain poverty and simplicity as the distinctive mark of the Friars Minor. He insisted on their having only the smallest houses to live in, and he encouraged them to observe strict rules about food and clothing. There is no doubt that they put up with a good deal of hardship and discomfort, that they tried to keep the vows which they had made, and that they wanted to carry out the wishes of their founder who had himself suffered so much. As Dr. Little says, 'certainly at first the friars in England revelled in poverty with a zest which may well have cheered the heart of St. Francis in his last sad days'. For this Agnellus was, no doubt, largely responsible. He was highly thought of by the King, who made use of his services on several occasions. It was while he was trying to settle a quarrel between the King and the Earl Marshall that he fell ill with dysentery, and died in Oxford in 1236.

He was succeeded as Provincial Minister by his friend Albert of Pisa, who had been, for some years, minister in Germany and parts of Italy. Albert was also a man of great self-discipline, a personal friend of St. Francis who had been so shocked at his abstinence that he ordered him to double the amount of food which he allowed himself to eat. Albert found, in England, a keen, dedicated group of men, and he was determined to maintain a high standard of discipline and poverty. He particularly stressed the importance of what we should now call the 'image' of the friars, insisting that, as they went about, they should look like men who had renounced the world and devoted their lives to the service of Lady Poverty. He was particularly angry if he thought the friars' buildings were too elaborate, and when he found a stone cloister being built at Southampton he ordered it to be pulled down, to the great indignation of the townsfolk who had paid for it to be built. At Reading he was prevented from demolishing the chapel which the friars had built because the money for this had been provided by the King. 'In that case' he said, 'I hope God will destroy it'.

In 1239, on the deposition of the notorious Brother Elias, Albert was elected Minister General of the Order, and was succeeded in England by Haymo of Faversham, who held office for only one year. Haymo was a fine scholar who, while lecturing in Paris, felt that he must throw in his lot with the Franciscans and joined the Order about 1225, coming, soon after this, to England in order to give lectures at Oxford. Haymo was typical of a group of early Franciscans who wanted to unite the zeal and austerity of the mendicant friars with the selflessness and discipline of the universities. He was a first class theologian and a renowned liturgist, and yet he always wore the scantiest clothing and sat on the ground in the refectory though suffering from constant ill-health. By the time he became Provincial Minister in England he had played a notable part in the internal affairs of the Order; had been sent by the pope on a mission to the Eastern Church, had led the opposition to Brother Elias, and had lectured at Bologna and Padua as well as at Paris and Oxford. He would, therefore, have done a great deal to help the friars in England had he stayed longer with them; but after only a year in office he succeeded Albert of Pisa as Minister General in 1240 and died at Anagni in 1244.

His successor in England, William of Nottingham, held office from 1240 to 1254. Nothing is known of his early life except that he was for a time a member of the Franciscan community in Rome where, he once said, he had eaten so many chestnuts that he was ashamed to see how fat he got. As Provincial Minister of England he encouraged the friars in all aspects of their work, especially in the study of theology; and it was in his time that the friary at Oxford was considerably enlarged. In 1254 he was sent on a mission to the pope, but, at Genoa, his companion was struck down by the plague. William stayed to look after him, caught the disease and died there almost immediately.

These four men—two Italians and two Englishmen—did much to establish the Order in England and to determine its features during the first thirty years from 1224 to 1254. During this time the country was divided into regions known as 'custodies' each with its own custos. There were at first, eight of these with their centres at London, Oxford, Bristol, Cambridge, Worcester, York, Newcastle and Salisbury, though the last was later joined with London. There were also six friaries in Scotland which were sometimes regarded as part of the province of England and sometimes not. By 1278 they became a more or less independent 'vicariate' and in 1329 were formally recognised as such.

The friars who formed the Franciscan Province of England were a very mixed lot. Some came from abroad, not only six of the original party but others after them, such as Albert of Pisa, Peter of Spain and William of Poitiers. But most of the friars were English by birth, though some had lived and worked abroad. They were of all classes. Some certainly belonged to the richer families—men with names like Robert Fitzwalter and Robert de Lisle; at least one, Ralph of Maidstone, had been a bishop (Hereford) and one, John of Reading, an abbot (Osney). Some were distinguished scholars and some intelligent young men from the universities. Others were of quite humble origin. The Order accepted them as they came, proud to have all kinds of men so long as they upheld the ideals that the friars stood for. It is difficult, in this early period, to know what proportion of the friars were in holy orders. The Order of Friars Minor was, in its origin, a predominently lay movement, though Innocent III had insisted on investing the first twelve friars with the tonsure and had made St. Francis a deacon. There were at first, few priests; but, as time went on, clericalisation gradually took place, and, from Albert of Pisa onwards, all Ministers General were priests.

As far as numbers go, we have not much evidence for the early days though there were known to be eighty friars in the London house in 1243, making it as large as the biggest Benedictine and Cistercian abbeys. At this time Winchester and Chichester each had about twenty-five members, and Reading thirteen. Eccleston tells us that in 1255 there were altogether 1,242 friars in England making an average of about twenty-five to each house. This means that, within thirty-two years, no less than forty-nine new religious houses had arisen in England, and these set up by only one of the four Orders of friars. As each was comparable in size to the average existing monastic community, the coming of the friars had introduced a new and influential element into the religious life of the country.

How this affected the life of the people of England we shall see shortly; but there is no doubt that, in these early days, the friars kept up a high standard of poverty and simplicity. Albert of Pisa once said that there were three things which brought special honour to the Order in England—bare feet, ragged clothing and hatred of money; and when the Minister General, John of Parma, came to England about 1250 he was immensely encouraged by what he saw, and said repeatedly: 'How I wish that a province such as this could be set in the centre of the world and provide an example to the whole Order'.

3

LIFE AND WORK OF THE FRIARS

At the death of St. Francis in 1226 there were really two
parties, or two policies, among the friars. There were
those who wanted to continue, without any kind of relax-
ation, the sort of life which the first friars had lived with
St. Francis himself. This meant that they had no settled
homes, that they were vagrants and beggars, working if
they could but otherwise totally dependent upon God
and upon the goodwill of their fellow-men. They walked,
barefoot, from village to village; they lived with the out-
casts and the lepers; they preached Christ and the Gospel
of renunciation not only in word but in deed; they were
prepared to go anywhere and do anything if they thought
God willed them to do so, even though it meant death by
exposure or at the hands of the Moslems.

On the other hand there were those who realised that
St. Francis had started something which was going to
grow and which would have to be controlled and organised. Conditions which could be accepted by a handful
of enthusiasts could not be imposed on thousands of
men living all over Europe in very varied conditions. What
began as a brotherhood had now become a religious Order,
with provinces, ministers, a Rule, chapter meetings and
all the planning which was necessary to run an institution
which contained many thousands of enthusiastic and often
intelligent and competent men. Francis' friend and adviser,
Ugolino, who, in due course, became pope as Gregory IX,
had seen this early on in the history of the movement, and
had angered some of the friars by his interference. But
Gregory was convinced that, if the Order was going to

flourish, and if it was going to be of service to the Church as a whole, then some measure of control was essential and inevitable. The friars must learn to live a more settled life. The priests who joined the Order, and those friars who were ordained after they had joined it, must have altars at which to say Mass, and breviaries out of which to say their offices. Simplicity was good and must always be preserved, but absolute poverty was impossible in an Order of this size. If the friars were going to be efficient preachers they must have books from which to prepare their sermons, and if they were good preachers they must have opportunities of delivering their message even if it meant building their own churches. If they were to play some part in the intellectual and academic movements of the time they must have opportunities for study. If they were to survive at all they must be prepared to receive some support from the Church authorities even if this meant accepting privileges from the Holy See.

So, after the death of St. Francis, and indeed during his lifetime, there was a struggle going on between two ideals. Some of the friars, who came to be called 'Spirituals' or 'Zealots' were all for simplicity, poverty and humility. They did not want papal support. They wanted to live as Francis had lived, believing that they would serve Christ better in this way than in any other. The other party, sometimes known as 'Conventuals' felt equally strongly that they could preserve the spirit of St. Francis, and maintain his ideals, while at the same time submitting to the authorities. After all, did not St. Francis promise obedience to the pope? How then could his followers refuse to do what the Holy See was clearly wanting them to do?

So the Order was not altogether united, and thus it remained for many years. But, so far as we know, these struggles did not effect the lives of the friars in England who seem to have been all of one mind. They certainly kept up high standards of poverty under the leadership of men like Agnellus and Albert of Pisa and their immediate successors. It is true that at Oxford considerable building took place between 1240 and 1250, but this was to meet the needs of the very flourishing theological school which they had started there. For the most part the friars, during this period, were content to live in small and often dilapidated houses, to tramp the country barefoot and ill-clad, to put up with a certain amount of ridicule and opposition from those who did not appreciate what they were trying to do.

But from about 1270 onwards, a good many changes took place. By this time the Order as a whole was developing its work and was erecting good monastic houses for the friars all over Europe. Some of the friars bitterly resented this; but men like St. Bonaventura, who was Minister General from 1257 to 1274 approved of it, and he defended his policy against all his critics. In large convents, he said, discipline is more easily enforced, opportunity can be provided for study and for the training of novices, and better worship can be offered. It was important, too, that the friars should allow themselves the use of books and vestments so long as, legally, they were the property of their friends outside the Order. Bonaventura saw no betrayal of Francis' ideals in the growing stability and security of the friars. He saw the Order as a great tool in the hands of the Church and he wanted to make it as efficient as possible.

So it was that, in England, things began to change. At Canterbury a friary was built with a church and most of the normal monastic buildings. At London the friars, who had been steadily adding bits of land to their site, started in 1279 on a big building programme which included a large church—300 feet long and 83 feet wide—with a number of side chapels. At Cambridge the friars left the House of Benjamin the Jew and built their own convent. At Exeter they moved to a new site in 1291, abandoning the very poor quarters which they had had up till then— so poor that the Earl of Hereford described the place as detestable while the stench was insupportable. And so it was all over the country as the friars began to build for themselves instead of putting up with makeshift accommo- dation. There were also, in the latter part of the thirteenth century, a number of new foundations—Richmond in 1257, Beverley, Boston and Dorchester in the 1260's, followed by seven or eight other foundations before the end of the century. Thus, by 1300, there were fifty-nine Franciscan houses in England to which four more were added in the fourteenth century at Walsingham, Plymouth, Aylesbury and Ware.

When new building schemes were being considered the friars had to think out carefully what they wanted. Their main need, apart from the domestic buildings, was a church where people could come, possibly in large numbers, to hear their sermons. Their churches, therefore, tended to be large, barn-like structures, unencumbered by pillars and screens, so as to accommodate as many people as possible. The remainder of the buildings depended very much on the shape and nature of the site. The monks had generally settled in rural areas where there was plenty of space, and their buildings tended to cover a good deal of land. These were surrounded by their estates—farms and manors—some of which they ran themselves and some of which they let. Any monastic cartulary will indicate the very extensive estates of the older religious houses.

But the friars built mostly in towns where the land was

precious, and their buildings had to be designed to fit the available space. This meant that no two Franciscan friaries were identical. If possible the friars liked to have a bit of a garden, for Haymo of Faversham had encouraged them to grow their own fruit and vegetables so as not to be too much dependent on others. But few of the friaries had any land for farming. Babwell, where the friars had settled after being driven out of Bury St. Edmunds, had the largest estate, amounting to forty-three acres, and Preston had about twenty acres; but most of the urban houses had to be content with four or five acres at the most.

Besides a church the friars would need a refectory and kitchen with the necessary store-rooms, a dormitory, a chapter-house and such other buildings—infirmary, guest-house, library, etc.—as they could afford or could fit into their site, the whole thing being normally surrounded by a wall. Few friars had private rooms, though these were allocated sometimes to the lectors who obviously needed some privacy. Nothing was normally set aside for the head of the community, the guardian, who had his meals with his fellow friars in the refectory and slept with them in the dormitory. Unlike the monasteries, where men were elected to offices which they held probably for life, and which were supported by their own manors and rents, the friaries were very democratic corporations which elected men to office for a year or two without cutting them off from the general life of the community.

As the friaries were mostly built in the towns there is not much left of them to-day; but what is left shows that they were generally built of fairly cheap material and not like the great monasteries. It was rather unkind of Matthew Paris to say that the friars' houses rivalled royal palaces when his own monastery of St. Alban's was far bigger than anything the friars ever built. Nevertheless there were several occasions when the King put up in one of the Franciscan houses, and Queen Isabella once entertained sixty ladies in the friars' dormitory at York.

Within the buildings the furniture also was simple. The only thing that the friars wanted to acquire in any quantity was books; and some of their libraries were undoubtedly fairly large. The library at Oxford was probably begun by Adam Marsh who had inherited a good collection of books from his uncle who was Bishop of Durham. We know, also, that, in 1253, Robert Grosseteste left his library to the Oxford Franciscans, though we have little indication as to how large it was. The Oxford friary had, in fact, two libraries, one for the students and the other for the rest of the convent; and at Cambridge there were three. Hereford and Exeter are known to have had good collections of books and the same was, no doubt, true of other places. The friars were, in fact, such keen book-buyers that Richard Fitzralph Archbishop of Armagh in 1357, said that 'in the faculties of the Arts, Theology, Canon Law and, as many assert, Medicine and Civil Law, scarcely a useful book is to be found in the market, but all are bought up by the friars'. But this may be an exaggeration, for Fitzralph was a very keen critic of the friars and of all that they did.

One thing which the friars took a lot of trouble about was their water-supply. Francis had praised 'Sister Water' which, he said, was 'useful, humble, precious and pure'; and the English friars were keen to get clean water in their houses. The water available in most towns was far from clean, and the friars made great efforts to build conduits which would bring in good, clear water from the country-side. The London friars built their aqueduct in 1255, Oxford about 1280 (with a gift of money from Edward I), and many others after that, including Cambridge where the friars built a conduit from a well near the Madingley

Road straight to their convent. This conduit eventually passed into the hands of Trinity College where it still supplies the water for the fountain in the Great Court.

Within these sixty convents lived a total population of between 1,000 and 1,700 friars. The total number fluctuated, being at its highest during the early years of the fourteenth century and falling considerably at the Black Death. It then rose a little but declined again in the sixteenth century in the years before the Dissolution. The population of each individual house also varied from time to time owing to the fact that so many of the friars were constantly on the move. The monk was bound by the vow of *stabilitas* to stay in one monastery for the whole of his life; but if the friar had taken any such vow it would have been of *mobilitas* as he was, essentially, an itinerant preacher. A house like Canterbury could vary between thirty and sixty, but this was perhaps because it lay on the Dover Road. Oxford, Cambridge and London were always the three largest houses with a population of anything up to eighty. Many houses kept to a fairly steady thirty to forty, and a few had no more than twenty. It was unusual to find a house with less than that until the eve of the Dissolution when a good many friars had made off for one reason or another.

Most of the friars were ordained. In some parts of Europe the friaries contained a good many lay-brothers, some of whom were, no doubt, employed in a domestic capacity. But there is no evidence of this in England where the numbers of unordained brothers was small. Of the 144 friars who died between 1328 and 1334 only nine were laymen, and the ordination lists in the bishops' registers suggest that most friars came up sooner or later for ordination, though not all, by any means, to the priest-hood. Many of them were young. The minimum age for entry into the Order was fixed in 1260 at eighteen, but, in 1316, it was reduced to fourteen. As boys went to the university at about this age some of them found the life of the friars very attractive and were duly professed during their student days. After the Black Death (1349) when so many friars, since they lived in the towns and ministered to the sick, caught the disease and died, it is possible that the Orders swept in a lot of boys to fill their ranks.

With no lands or estates or rents the friars had to support themselves as best they could. At first they had either earned their food or begged it from door to door. But, as time went on, other sources of income were found. Some friaries acquired a little property from which rents could be drawn, but this never amounted to much. Many of the friaries received gifts from the King, sometimes in cash, sometimes in kind. The Oxford and Cambridge houses both had grants from the Exchequer which were paid fairly regularly right up to the Dissolution. Edward I adopted the habit of giving a groat (4d) a day to each friar in the places through which he passed—a convenient way of discovering the numbers of friars there at the time. Some friars received gifts for services rendered, especially in saying masses for the dead or in burial fees, and some earned money by their skill—such as the friar who repaired the organs in York Minster in 1485. A few friars had small private incomes, though this was strictly contrary to the Rule, and a good many received presents from relatives to enable them to buy books or to get a new habit. In later years one or two friars like John Bosgawyn, 'of gentle blood and a renowned preacher' received a dispensation to hold a benefice, though this would not, of course, carry with it any pastoral responsibility.

In later years the communities received a good deal of property, both financial and otherwise, in legacies. Hundreds of wills are known to have contained gifts to the friars, for, although people often criticised the friars, they continued to believe in them and to value their prayers. Some of the richer benefactors were buried in the Franciscan churches, no less than 765 tombs having been recorded in the friars' church in London.

But, for the most part, the friars depended upon what we should now call 'voluntary subscriptions'. As there was no general postal system, these had to be collected, and a system was devised whereby the country adjacent to the friary was divided up into regions, known as 'limitations', and certain friars, called 'limitors' were given the task of going regularly to houses in their region to collect the gifts. The limitors sometimes acquired a reputation for fraud and dishonesty, like Chaucer's friar of Holderness who, in return for the gifts which he received, wrote down the names of donors with promises to pray for them, yet, as soon as he was out of sight 'planed out the names everychoon'. But not all of them behaved like this, or they would have been found out and this source of income would soon have dried up.

According to the Rule, friars were forbidden to touch money or to receive it in any form either personally or through an intermediary. This was just possible in the early days when the friars wandered about and threw themselves on the hospitality of the people whom they served. But it became impossible when the Order grew large, and we soon find a system growing up of 'spiritual friends' who looked after the money which was paid in. This, however, did not last very long, as many of the friars wanted to manage their own affairs. A few tried to observe the letter of the law by counting the money with gloves on, or with a stick, and some took boys round with them so that they could actually handle the money; but this was seen to be dishonest, and it was not long before this particular injunction in the Rule came to be regarded as obsolete.

As early as 1260 the friars had passed a resolution that proper accounts should be kept in each community and that these should be presented at chapter-meetings from time to time. Whether or not his was observed we do not know, as very little has survived to give us much idea of how the friars looked after their financial affairs. The one surviving fragment of an account-book turned up in the binding of a Greek Psalter at Cambridge some years ago. There is no doubt that it came from the Franciscan house in Cambridge and that it belonged to the years 1363—66. It is not really an account-book as income and expenditure are all mixed up. What it appears to be is part of a note-book in which were written down the amounts given by various well-wishers, mostly in the form of money, but sometimes in kind, such as figs, herrings and pork. The amounts of money vary considerably; and as there is nothing recorded less than 6d. it looks as if a lot of smaller gifts were not entered into the book. It has been suggested that the friars' income from this source would be about £1 a week, or enough to support fifteen friars.

The friars who arrived at Dover in 1224 were bare-footed and wearing patched and shabby tunics. So poor did they look that they were immediately mistaken for rogues and vagabonds. Such very simple clothing con-tinued to be the lot of the friars. Their habits were made of coarse cloth of nondescript colour which was mostly grey though perhaps with some brown in it. The habit had a hood attached to it and was gathered together by a knotted cord. The practice of going barefoot was maintained for some years, but was gradually discontinued.

The friars regarded themselves as missionaries and evangelists. But they were also members of religious communities, and were expected to say the offices daily. Some of them carried breviaries about with them so that, even if they were on the road, they could say their prayers. For this purpose very small and light breviaries were made, one which has survived weighing less than five ounces although bound in leather. Their Sunday services were open to the public and, if a sermon was being preached, they often attracted large numbers. Within the house many of the brothers, priests as well as laymen, would be occupied in the maintenance of the community by getting food, perparing it for their meals and seeing to the upkeep and cleanliness of the buildings. Some would work in the garden while others, especially the students, would read in the cloister or the library.

As they went about the country they sought every opportunity of preaching whether in their own church, the parish churches, or in the open air. Robert Grosseteste told Gregory IX that the Franciscans in England 'illuminate our whole country with the bright light of their preaching and teaching'. They were generally supported and encouraged by the bishops, who realised that the friars could often make up what was lacking in the ministry of the parish priests. The friars made preaching one of their special tasks, and trained and prepared themselves for it. There are no records of outstanding preachers in England like Antony of Padua whose preaching drew such large crowds that all the shops closed when he was in the pulpit since trade was at a standstill. Nor were there any who could be compared with Berthold of Regensberg who attracted such large crowds to his open-air services that he used to fly a little flag to show which way the wind was blowing so that people would know where to go if they wished to hear him. There was certainly no English friar of this class but there is no doubt that they were popular and that their sermons were appreciated.

Franciscan sermons were generally vivid, sometimes witty, and often very outspoken. The preachers not only expounded the Scriptures—sometimes with considerable flights of imagination—they denounced injustices and moral failings and gave their views on political and social issues.

They were also employed sometimes to preach on behalf of the Crusades or to stir people up to support the war against the Scots. Their sermons were spiced with descriptions of foreign parts which they had visited, with popular songs, and with stories, fables and illustrations from the books of *exempla* which were written for their use. One of these books, called *Dormi Secure* or *Sleep Soundly*, was intended to ensure that a preacher could go safely to bed on Saturday night since the book would give him plenty of material out of which to put up a sermon on Sunday morning. Archbishop Pecham called the friars 'the wheels of God's chariot', carrying God's message through the land. At a time when sermons in parish churches were generally few and inclined to be dull, the friars certainly filled a gap in the Church's ministry.

With the sermons went pastoral care and counselling. The friars preached in such a way that a good many people wanted to consult them afterwards or to make their confessions. When Haymo of Faversham preached in Paris one day, the number of penitents was so great that he had to sit in the church for three whole days in order to deal with them.

There is not much written evidence of the friars working much among the sick and the poor, though there is little doubt that some of them were occupied in this way. That they knew something of the problems of the poor and where help was needed is proved by the fact that Gregory Rokesle, who had been several times Mayor of London left his estate for the poor with instructions that it was to be administered by the Friars Minor of London and Canterbury. But there is no evidence of their doing the sort of thing which was later done in Italy, where the Franciscans set up the lending banks known as the *Monti di Pietá* to try and help the poorer farmers.

Not all the friars were confined to their houses, or went on preaching tours, or worked among the poor. Some played a considerable part in the life of the country, occasionally risking their safety and their reputation by supporting an unpopular cause. In 1256 certain Jews were accused of having kidnapped and crucified a boy at Lincoln. Feeling ran very high, and when seventy-one Jews were condemned to death there was much jubilation. The condemned Jews somehow managed to get secret messages to the friars who took up their cause and eventually got them reprieved. This was certainly a very unpopular move and cost the friars considerable support. But it was a courageous and self sacrificing course to take. About the same time Adam Marsh and other Franciscans took up the cause of Simon de Montfort against the King, again earning for themselves a good deal of criticism and reproach. In later years some of the friars took a very active part in the trial of John Wyclif, but this was not surprising in view of the attacks which he had made upon them.

The Franciscans were a very cosmopolitan lot, and their work often took them far from home. A good many foreign friars made their way to England for one thing or another, mostly to study at either Oxford or Cambridge. In 1336

Benedict XII ruled that, every third year, the friars' lector at the universities should be from overseas. The ruling was not strictly observed, but, as a result of it, a number of continental scholars came and spent a year at one of the English universities lecturing to the friers. In addition to the lecturers we also find a number of foreign students not only in the universities but in most of the friaries up and down the country. Many of them came from Germany, and we have records of at least sixty-six Franciscans from Cologne who came to live in England. A number of very distinguished friars also came over— men like Leonardo di Giffono who became Minister General of the Order in 1373, and Peter Philargi from Crete who eventually became pope as Alexander V.

In the same way a number of English friars went to work or to study abroad and their names keep cropping up in university registers, chronicles and other sources. A few, following in the footsteps of St. Francis, went further afield as missionaries. Richard of Ingworth, having helped to found the English province went out to the Holy Land and died there. His contemporary, Adam of Oxford, also went out to preach to the Moslems. Others went, in some capacity or other, with the Crusaders; and one, William Walden, was martyred in Persia in 1342.

4

THE SECOND AND THIRD ORDERS

In the year 1212 St. Francis preached a number of sermons in the church of San Rufino, which is the cathedral church of Assisi. Among those who came to listen to these sermons was a girl of about eighteen years of age called Clare, the daughter of one of the wealthy Assisian families. Clare was, not unnaturally, extremely moved by these sermons and found some opportunity of talking to Francis about what he had been saying. There is some evidence that Francis encouraged her to do more for the poor, and even to go out in disguise and find out what it felt like to be a beggar with no knowledge of where your next meal was to come from. Clare may well have expressed some desire to do what Francis was doing —that is, to renounce all that she had and join the friars in their evangelism and poverty. Whether this was so or not, Francis told her to escape from her house on the evening of Palm Sunday and make her way down the hill to the Portiuncula. This she did, and when she got there he invited her to take vows somewhat similar to those made by the friars. He then cut off her hair and clothed her in some rough garments.

As soon as he had done this he began to wonder what he was going to do with her. Obviously she could not become a member of a band of wandering preachers, and the only thing to do was to find a religious house which would take her in. After two short periods in local Benedictine nunneries, Clare, together with her sister Agnes and one or two other young ladies, was installed in the buildings belonging to the church of San Damiano, not far from the city. And here Clare lived for the rest of her life. Gone then were the dreams of going about with the friars, of serving the poor, of going out as a missionary and perhaps winning the much-coveted crown of martyrdom.

The followers of St. Clare, at first known as 'the Poor Ladies of San Damiano', were, from the beginning, an order of enclosed nuns, with no opportunity of doing any practical work among their fellows. They lived a life of great austerity and discipline, for the standard of living was kept very low. At all times completely cut off from the world, they devoted their lives to prayer and manual work. But this form of life clearly appealed to others, for the Order grew fairly rapidly and houses were founded first in Italy and then in France, Bohemia and elsewhere.

The members of what came to be called the 'Second Order' did not all keep the same Rule. Clare had her own Rule at San Damiano, and those who adopted it were called 'Damianites'. There were two other Rules, both based on Benedictine models, one for the nuns of Long-champs, near Paris, and one given to the sisters by Urban IV. The latter were called 'Clarisses', the former 'Minoresses'.

In addition to those who were members of the Second Order there were also some groups of women who wanted to adopt the life of mendicancy and service which had been denied to St. Clare. Some of these groups were known to have started up in England in the 1240s. This is not surprising, as the friars had by then been in England for about twenty years and had inspired many people by their preaching and example. It was, therefore, not unnatural that some enterprising young women might have wanted to do something similar, and their experiments won the admiration of many people, including the chronicler, Roger of Wendover. But the Church did not approve of spontaneous movements of this sort; and, in 1250, Innocent IV sent a letter to the English bishops warning them to prevent women going about calling themselves 'Sisters Minor'. Those who did so might appear outwardly virtuous, but were inwardly mischievous. The bishops seem to have done what they were told to do, and we hear no more of these groups.

The first official house of Franciscan nuns was started at Northampton, where, in 1252, Henry III ordered the sheriff to provide them with five habits. But the community does not seem to have flourished, and, within twenty years, it had ceased to exist. Soon after this, in 1286, a Northumbrian nobleman, called John de Vescy, bought a house in Newcastle-on-Tyne from the Friars of the Sack and tried to found a house of Franciscan sisters there, but without success.

Meanwhile, a wealthy lady called Denise de Munchesney was making plans for setting up two houses of Minoresses, one of which was to be in London and the other at her manor of Waterbeach, near Cambridge. The plan was delayed for some years; but, in 1293, a small community of sisters was set up in London, and, in the following year, four sisters came from France to establish a house at Waterbeach. The nunnery at Waterbeach was Denise's own foundation, while that in London owed its existence to the generosity of Blanche, Queen of Navarre and wife of Edmund, Earl of Lancaster, the brother of Edward I.

With the disappearance of the house at Northampton about 1272 there were only these two houses of Minoresses in England until 1342 when Mary de St.Pol started making plans for the establishment of a house at Denney which was intended to replace the one at Waterbeach. Mary of St.Pol had aquired, in 1336, a small monastery

43

at Denney which had been occupied by various communities, including the Knights Templars and the Hospitallers. As this was a better building, and on a much better site than the house at Waterbeach, she obtained licence, in 1339, to move the whole community to the new house. In 1342 the abbess and most of the sisters agreed to do this. But about twenty of the sisters refused to leave their home, elected their own superior, and tried to continue as an independent community. For nine years the two communities existed side by side and there was a good deal of recrimination and ill-will. But in 1351, after the Black Death had perhaps carried off some of the more troublesome members, all but three of the sisters submitted and went over to Denney. Attempts were made to turn the empty buildings into a friary, but nothing came of this.

Shortly after this, between 1364 and 1367, a third house was founded at Bruisyard in Suffolk by Lionel, Duke of Clarence. Lionel was anxious to find a home for his mother-in-law, Maud, Countess of Ulster. About twenty years earlier, this old lady had set up a chantry for five priests at Campsey Ash, in Suffolk, close to a house of Augustinian canonesses of which she herself was a member. But the priests who went there disliked the place so much that they persuaded Maud to transfer the chantry to Bruisyard. This she did, but the priests misbehaved. They kept no rule, neglected the services, and went about in secular clothes. Maud disapproved of this, and, after a year or two, had them removed. She then turned the chantry into a house of Minoresses, and thirteen sisters went there from Denney to start it off. After this two further attempts were made to found houses of Franciscan nuns, one at Hull and the other at

Clovelly, but neither succeeded, and there remained only the three monasteries in London, Denney and Bruisyard.

There is no doubt that, inspite of the wishes of St. Clare, the sisters soon came to acquire a good deal of property. The London sisters certainly owned a number of dwelling-places in the city from which they drew considerable rents. The rural convents complained continuously of their poverty, but Denney owned a good deal of land, including four manors, and four appropriated churches from which they collected the benefice endowments while paying vicars a much smaller sum to look after the parishes. All the three houses were supported by noble families, many of whom had relatives there. Novices were expected, as in most monasteries, to bring some money with them; and the nuns also received legacies and gifts of various kinds. The London sisters certainly got a good deal of support from merchants in the city. Some Franciscan nunneries were founded exclusively for members of the nobility, and young ladies of a lower class were not eligible for membership; but there is no evidence of this in the English houses.

The Second Order depended very much on the First. Shut up in their convents the sisters needed the friars to raise money for them and to act as their chaplains, confessors and legal and financial advisors. The sisters had no internal organisation and no chapters or regular meetings. They were known sometimes as 'sisters of the Order of Friars Minor' and their superiors were the general and provincial ministers who managed the affairs of the friars. The heads of houses, known as abbesses, had no official means of meeting together to discuss their problems. They were expected, together with the sisters who were in their care, to live useful and quiet lives in their convents and not to worry about what was going on outside. Each convent had one of the friars as its visitor, and it was usual to have resident friars to act as chaplains and the Provincial Minister was expected to look in on them from time to time to see that all was well. Lay people were seldom admitted to these convents though a few managed to gain admittance in order to see their relatives. There were, however, as in most religious houses, a number of *corrodars*, that is men and women who were housed for considerable periods. They would either bring their own servants to look after them or would be waited on by the servants employed by the convent. Most religious houses in those days had armies of servants to look after them. The nuns of Denney employed a chef in the kitchen with a boy to do the more menial jobs.

These three communities of Poor Clares or Minoresses were, therefore, very like the other houses of sisters scattered about all over the country. London and Denny each contained about 25 sisters, but Bruisyard considerably less. The ladies lived a quiet, retired, disciplined life, devoted to work and prayer. Like all nunneries these houses provided security, sufficient comfort, and the assurance of medical care in old age. Life was monotonous, and there was little change as the years went by, for there is no sign in England of the reforming movement inaugurated in France by St. Colette in the fourteenth century.

In addition to founding the Friars Minor and the Minoresses, Francis also inaugurated what was at first called the 'Order of Penitence' but which came to be known as the 'Third Order'. This was intended for clergy and lay people who, for one reason or another, could not be enrolled in one of the other Orders. St. Francis was anxious to draw into a fellowship those who wished to live a life of simplicity and of discipline, who were willing to observe certain rules, and who wanted to set a good example to the world. Members of this fellowship lived in their own houses and carried out their responsibilities in their families; but they took certain vows and had their own officers who were called ministers, bursars, chaplains and so forth. Some of these communities in the towns acquired a certain amount of property, especially rooms in which they could hold their meetings and churches in which they could gather for worship.

But as time went by, some of these groups felt that they wanted more co-ordination and more organisation. Unmarried women or widows would get hold of a house and live together as a small community, and some men did the same. Once they had started to do this it was not long before they became more monastic. They drew up a strict rule of life, they took vows, they wore habits, and the women adopted the custom of the Minoresses and became contemplative and enclosed. In time, therefore, the word 'tertiary' could mean two quite different things. It could mean people living at home and pursuing their own occupations, yet pledged to standards of simplicity and integrity—much like members of any Church Guild or Fellowship today. But the word could also mean a member of an enclosed community with strict rules and customes, differing very little from friars or Minoresses.

There were no establishments of tertiaries in England, though a house of Grey Sisters was set up at Aberdour in 1486 and another at Dundee in 1502. But there were certainly some members of the Third Order in the more general sense, though probably not very many. There was, for example, a priest called Samson de Brocke who had a parish in Lincolnshire who, in 1355, received a plenary indulgence when he was dying. Another, called Alexander, a member of the Third Order in London, died in 1486. But, apart from these two, nothing is known of any groups of tertiaries in England. It is possible that one or two hermits and anchoresses, like Margaret of Richmond, may have adopted the Rule of the Third Order, as she received her habit from the friars and left her goods to them in 1490. Katherine of Aragon was also a tertiary. But beyond that there is little to record.

On the other hand, some people found other ways of associating themselves with the friars. One was by applying for 'Letters of Fraternity'. These go back to the thirteenth century and became fairly common in later years. The system was that, on payment of a sum of money, or for services rendered, a man or woman might be given a letter of Fraternity which meant that the applicant would be inscribed as a *confrater* or *consoror*, and that he or she would be prayed for after death. This was something which could obviously be abused and turned into little more than a money-making device; but in its intentions it was good. The first known Letter of Fraternity issued in England was given to a man called Thomas of Macclesfield in 1301. Some of the letters were issued by the Minister General, some by the Provincial Ministers or local guardians, but all carried certain privileges with them.

One of these privileges was to be buried in a Franciscan habit, in hopes (presumably) of being mistaken for a faithful follower of St. Francis on arrival at the gates of heaven. Several effigies are still in existence, including one at Conington in Huntingdonshire dating from about the year 1300. Mary of St. Pol was buried in a habit at the nunnery which she had founded at Denney. Privileges of this kind were much sought after, and dearly bought; with the result that the practice came in for a certain amount of criticism from people like Wyclif and Langland. But the system showed that there were people in England who wished to be associated with the friars even though they may not have formed into congregations of tertiaries.

5

THE FRIARS AND SCHOLARSHIP

There is no reason to suppose that St. Francis disapproved of scholarship. Indeed he always showed great respect and reverence towards men of learning. But he did not want his friars to engage in scholarly pursuits since he thought that this would be incompatible with the kind of life which he wanted them to live— a life based on the three principles of poverty, simplicity and humility. The Friar Minor was to serve the poor and the outcast; and, if he preached, it was to be a simple appeal to people to love God and to renounce sin. A high level of scholarship was not necessary for this kind of life, and might well spoil it. Scholars needed books, and the possession of books was incompatible with poverty. They were inclined to get involved in learned discussions and disputations which would militate against simplicity. They were also likely to get conceited and regard themselves as superior to less-educated men, and this would mar their humility. When, therefore, St. Francis saw what he regarded as signs that the friars were trying to turn his Order into a learned institution like the Order of Preachers, he soon showed his disapproval. For example, when he arrived once at Bologna and found that the local Minister (himself a learned man and doctor of law) had built or adapted a house so that it could serve as a place of study, he refused to enter it and went off to stay with the Dominicans.

It was obvious that while St. Francis was alive nothing much could be done. But during his lifetime and immediately after his death a good many men entered the Order, especially in the university towns, who wanted not only to pursue their studies, but also to use their knowledge for the welfare of mankind, both by their preaching and in other ways. Heresy was very much alive in Europe, and some of the friars were anxious to play their part in fighting it.

But why, it may be asked, did such men join the Order of Friars Minor? Would it not have been better if they had attached themselves to one of the older Orders, or to the Order of Preachers which existed for this very purpose? The probable answer is that they found the Order of St. Francis to be a very lively and vigorous community. It existed for the benefit of mankind and appealed to all that was good and adventurous in young men. It thus came about that, within a few years, the Order had enrolled a number of very learned and scholarly men, and was itself building up a system whereby its members could receive the best education that could be given.

We have seen how the friars who arrived in England in 1224 wasted very little time in making their way to Oxford, and, soon afterwards, to Cambridge. In those early days, with St. Francis still alive, they probably had no desire to play any part in the life of a university, but chose these towns because they knew them to be full of young men, some of whom might wish to become friars. But it was not long before they set up their own school at Oxford, based very largely on what they saw happening at Paris. Agnellus of Pisa was not a profound scholar, but he had spent some time at Paris, where he had seen the very good relationships which had been created there between the friars and the students. In 1225 four doctors of the University of Paris joined the Order of Friars Minor, including two Englishmen—Haymo of Faversham and Simon of Sandwich. Regular lectures, at university level, came to be regarded as one of the most natural parts of the friars' life. Another of the friars, an Englishman called Bartholomew, who had lectured on the Bible at Paris, was then sent off to teach the friars in Germany.

Seeing how well things were going in Paris, Agnellus decided to set up a school of theology at Oxford. There were already in the house a number of scholars—probably including men like Adam Marsh, Haymo of Faversham and Adam Rufus—any one of whom would have made an admirable lecturer. But Agnellus decided to approach the most distinguished scholar in Oxford, Robert Grosseteste, who had already shown his appreciation of what the friars were doing. So, about 1229, a building was put up in which lectures could be given and Grosseteste took up his work. Naturally a man of his calibre attracted very large numbers of students, and the Franciscan school became one of the most popular places in the university. Besides the secular students who went to these lectures, friars came sometimes from considerable distances, one chronicler describing them as walking many miles 'barefoot in bitter cold and deep mud' in order to hear Grosseteste's lectures. It is not known for certain what he lectured on, but it is probable that one of his most important works, *Moralities on the Gospel* may well be based on his lectures to the friars since these were worked out for the benefit of preachers.

Grosseteste continued as the friars' 'lector' until 1235 when he was made Bishop of Lincoln, and he was succeeded by three other lecturers, all secular priests, who presided over the school for the next ten years or so. Only when the school was well established, and had trained a number of learned friars, did a member of the Order take charge. This was Adam Marsh, a scholarly man who had been one of Grosseteste's pupils. He had been a parish priest in the diocese of Durham before he joined the Friars Minor about 1228. After teaching for a few years in Italy he came to Oxford as the head of the friars' school, and from then onwards all the lectors were members of the Order. Adam Marsh was a good scholar and teacher who did much for the Oxford friars; but nothing that he wrote has survived except a magnificent collection of 246 letters. Besides being a good teacher he was also a man of affairs who played an important part in the life of the Church and the State. He was a member of several commissions appointed to settle disputes in the Order and he carried out various tasks for the Pope, for the Archbishop of Canterbury, and for the King. As lector at Oxford he was succeeded by a number of distinguished men, including Thomas of York, Richard Rufus of Cornwall, John of Wales, Roger Marston and many others, most of whom have left some of their works behind them.

By the time that Adam Marsh took over the friars' Studium at Oxford, things were beginning to happen at Cambridge. Soon after the friars got established there they decided to follow the example of the Oxford convent and set up a school of theological teaching. At Oxford the friars had been able to draw on the masters in the faculty of theology, but there was, as yet, no such faculty at Cambridge. This meant that all the lectors there were friars, beginning with Vincent of Coventry who was succeeded by a French friar called William of Poitou. Thus whereas, at Oxford, the faculty of theology had helped to establish the friars' school, at Cambridge it was the friars who helped to set up a faculty of theology in the University.

The Franciscan lectors at Oxford and Cambridge were appointed by the friars; but they ranked as official teachers in the University, and secular scholars were encouraged to attend their lectures. This was all right at first, but led to some tension as time went by and the Universities became better organised. The best Franciscan lecturers were men of international reputation who attracted large numbers of students. But neither they, nor the friar-students whom they taught, were subject to university discipline or authority. For example, the University of Oxford had a rule that no one could proceed to the degree of Master of Theology unless he had first graduated in Arts. But the friars did not put their students through the Arts course since they had already received a good grounding before coming to University. The matter flared up on 1253 when the friars presented one of their most able students, Thomas of York, for a degree in Theology. This the University refused to grant since he had not graduated in Arts. Everyone recognised Thomas' ability and qualifications, but the statutes made it impossible for him to take his degree. The only solution was for the University, which could not afford to lose the friars' school with its learned professors, to grant special graces for any worthy students who presented themselves for degrees. At first things seem to have worked out reasonably well. The faculties of theology were in their early stages, and the Universities were fully aware of the contribution which the friars were making. But the friars felt aggrieved, since the University always had the power of witholding the necessary dispensation if it chose to do so; and, on various occasions, they tried to get the King or the Pope or some other influential person to support their claim to be the final judge of a man's competence.

Secular students usually came up to the University at the age of fourteen and spent seven years before graduating in Arts, after which they could, if they so wished, proceed to the study of theology. As friars did not read the Arts course they had to go through a period of preparation before coming to the University. This they would do in one of their own houses so that when they arrived at Oxford or Cambridge they were more or less qualified to read for a higher degree. The men sent to the Universities were those selected by the Provincial Minister because of their ability and many who would like to have taken a degree in Divinity, were not allowed to do so. Nevertheless the educational opportunity presented to the friars was considerable. Eccleston tells us that in 1254 there were in England thirty lecturers in the Franciscan convents who 'solemnly disputed' (i.e. taught at a high level) together with three or four others who lectured without disputations. This shows that there were a good many Franciscan schools up and down the country where good teaching was being given. This continued for some time; for when, in 1336, Benedict XII raised twenty-one Franciscan schools to a higher rank and made them colleges of advanced study, no less than one third of the total number so honoured were in England—at London, York, Norwich, Newcastle, Stamford, Coventry and Exeter.

We can see, therefore, a three-tier system in English Franciscan education. The friar began his studies in his own convent under the tuition of one of his fellows who was called *lector*. In due course he would be sent to one of the more advanced schools.

Finally, if he proved himself, he would go on to Oxford or Cambridge and read for his degree in theology like other post-graduate students. Indeed, so good was the friars' educational system that some of the friars were invited to lecture elsewhere, as when, from 1275 to 1314, a series of friars lectured to the monks of Christ Church, Canterbury, a pleasant repayment for the hospitality given to the first friars in 1224.

The English province of the Friars Minor produced a

number of very remarkable scholars: and it is interesting to note that out of the five most learned Franciscans of the thirteenth and early fourteenth centuries, no less than four were British—Alexander of Hales, Roger Bacon, Duns Scotus and William of Ockham. The fifth was an Italian, Bonaventura.

Alexander of Hales, known as *doctor irrefragabilis* was a Gloucestershire man and a leading theologian at Paris where he did much to build up the faculty of theology. Then, at the height of his power and influence, probably in the year 1236, he decided to join the friars and transfer his lectures to their school. This caused something of a sensation in the University since the friars' school was not under their jurisdiction. Alexander was thus the father of the Franciscan schoolmen, though he did not, so far as we know, return to England. He died in 1245 leaving his Summa Theologica unfinished. He was the first medieval writer to try to form a synthesis between reason and revelation, between Aristotle and the Bible, and it is on the foundations which he laid that much medieval philosophy was built.

Roger Bacon, *doctor mirabilis*, was a very different kind of man. He was born at Ilchester about 1214; studied at Oxford; and at some point joined the Order of Friars Minor. For some years he taught at Paris; but, about 1247, he resigned his chair and devoted himself to original research into physical, biological and mathematical as well as philosophical, theological and linguistic affairs. His works, which now fill 23 volumes, dealt with all kinds of subjects, as his fertile and penetrating mind occupied itself with every aspect of human knowledge. He is generally thought to have made an early type of telescope, and he is also credited with having discovered gun-powder, though, realising how dangerous this might be, he hid the formula in an anagram which has only recently been deciphered. Bacon was a man who was interested in everything, while, at the same time, critical of those who were content to turn out other people's ideas without really thinking them through. Bacon, as would be expected, had to face a lot of criticism during his lifetime; but after his death he acquired a great reputation, mingled with a certain amount of awe. He is still highly thought of since he is regarded as the forerunner of the experimental and scientific approach to knowledge.

John Duns Scotus, the *doctor subtilis* was born about 1265 and joined the friars at Dumfries. We know very little of his life, though he certainly taught at Oxford, Paris and Cambridge. He died at Cologne in 1308 and is buried there. Although there is some doubt of the authenticity of some of the writings which bear his name, he is generally recognised as one of the greatest of the medieval schoolmen. He had an independent mind and did much to guide the procedure of medieval scholasticism into a slightly different course from that set by his Dominican contemporary, Thomas Aquinas. Duns Scotus was very much disliked by the Reformers who thought him largely responsible for an over-exaltation of the character and role of the Virgin Mary. When the medieval libraries were being solemnly burnt in the sixteenth century the works of Duns Scotus were often the first to be put on the fire, and this refined and elegant thinker actually gave his name to the English word, 'dunce'—the least appropriate of all nicknames. Today, however, the writings and the thought of Duns Scotus are being taken very seriously by students of medieval philosophy.

The fourth English scholar, William of Ockham, the *doctor invincibilis*, really belongs to a later generation since he was not born until about the year 1300. Ockham

studied and lectured at Oxford but in such a way as to
arouse a certain amount of suspicion, for he was a liberal
and unorthodox thinker. So radical were some of his
views that he was summoned to the papal court at Avignon
to give some account of himself. Here he found a group
of fellow-friars from other parts of Europe, who were
arguing over the question of the meaning of poverty with
a view to carrying out some necessary reforms in the
Order. Ockham immediately joined forces with them,
and it was not long before they all found themselves in
prison for having criticised some of the pronouncements
of the pope, John XXII. They escaped, however, from
the prison and sailed to Italy where Ockham devoted
himself, with the utmost vigour, to theologico-political
and controversial writing. He was a man with a very
keen mind and was naturally critical of all existing schools
of thought. The theories which he supported, commonly
known as 'Nominalism' helped to break up some of the
established beliefs and conventions on which medieval
Church and State existed, so preparing the way for the
big changes which took place two hundred years later.

These four scholars were the greatest of the English
Franciscan theologians and philosophers. But there were
a great many others whose works were widely read and
whose names were remembered with respect, men like
John Pecham, Roger Marston, Bartholomew Glanville,
William Woodford, Walter of Chatton and many others.
One of the Cambridge friars, Henry of Costesy, who
died in 1336, was a biblical scholar of the first rank and
one of the few men of his age to study Hebrew, as well
as Greek and Latin, in order the better to understand
the Scriptures.

Apart from the work of theologians and philosophers
the English Franciscans turned out a good deal of litera-

ture of importance. There were first of all the chroniclers. Our knowledge of the first 25 years of the Order in England is based largely on the Chronicle written by a friar called Thomas of Eccleston. A native of Lancashire he studied in Oxford and lived for a time in London. He spent many years collecting material for his book, which is a splendid account of the coming of the friars and of their early years in England with a number of pen-portraits of interesting men. Whenever it is possible to check his statements from another source he is found to be accurate and reliable in what he says. He wrote for the edification of his fellow friars; but he has left us a source book of prime authority.

Some years later two Franciscan friars, one called Richard of Durham (or, possibly, Richard of Slekeburn) compiled a work which came to be known as the *Lanercost Chronicle*. This is intended to be a general history from 1201 onwards, but it contains some interesting information about the friars. It derives its name from the fact that in later years the manuscript fell into the hands of the Augustinian canons of Lanercost in Cumberland, who added a few notes about their own history. But the Chronicle is essentially a Franciscan production.

The friars were, as we have seen, great preachers who liked to salt their sermons with stories, fables, incidents of many kinds, many of them of a miraculous nature. It was undoubtedly the use of illustrative material—whether true or imaginery—which made the friars' sermons so popular and lured the people away from the parish churches into the friaries. In order to provide preachers with the sort of material which they wanted several books were written. One of these is the *Liber Exemplorum,* a collection of illustrative material, written by an English

Franciscan between 1275 and 1279. This contains 213 stories which are divided into two sections, one dealing with doctrine and the other with morals. In the following century a Norfolk friar called Nicholas Bozon wrote his *Contes Moralisés*. Nicholas wrote a good deal of stuff, both prose and poetry, and mostly in French. He was, himself, a gifted and attractive preacher, and wrote to help others to do well in this field. Another English friar, called John Grimestone, put together a commonplace book in 1372. This also was intended to provide material for preachers.

St. Francis himself was a poet, whose *Canticle of the Sun* is one of the earliest poems written in a modern language. Many of his followers also wrote poetry, some in Latin and some in the vernacular. John Pecham has already been mentioned as a theologian and teacher. He was also an administrator who became Provincial Minister of England, and, in 1279, Archbishop of Canterbury. But he was also a poet whose allegorical poem on the nightingale, called *Philomena*, is a work of great dignity and beauty, telling of the little songster who, as death approaches, sings all night with increasing passion until, as day breaks, she falls dead to the ground. The poem is intended to represent the Christian soul yearning for its heavenly country.

Philomena was written in Latin, and could appeal, therefore, only to the educated. But the friars' target was always the ordinary man, and much of their poetry was written in English with a view to quoting it (or singing it) in their sermons. Hence the composition of such things as the *Luue Ron* by Thomas of Hales which warns mankind of the fickleness of life and the danger of expecting too much from this world. This was written about 1275; but we know of little else of this kind until the fifteenth century when a friar of Canterbury, called James Ryman, produced a number of poems designed for preachers and others. No less than 166 of these have survived, some in English, some using both English and Latin. Most of them tell of the life of Christ or of his Virgin Mother in a simple way which audiences would understand.

One of the main objects of the Franciscan preachers was to help people to see the life of Christ as something which really happened, and to treat the narrations of the Gospel as historical rather than as symbolic or allegorical. For this reason, one of the most popular books in England was the work known as *Meditations on the Life of Christ* originally attributed to St. Bonaventura, but now known to be by an Italian friar called John de Caulibus. This proved to be very useful for preachers, as, not only did it recount the Gospel narrative in a most vivid way, but also enlarged upon them out of the fertile imagination of the writer. John de Caulibus wrote in Latin, but translations were quickly made. An English poet, called Robert Manning of Brunne, translated some of the Passion stories about 1320, and other parts were put into English by Nicholas Love, a Carthusian of Mount Grace in Yorkshire.

In spite, therefore, of St. Francis' warnings against the friars becoming scholastically-minded, his followers, in England as elsewhere, played an important part in the academic and literary life of the world. The faculties of theology at both Oxford and Cambridge owe much to the Franciscans, even if some of the greatest scholars from England did most of their teaching elsewhere. English literature also owes something to the friars in their preaching and in their efforts to make the Gospel vivid and intelligible to the simple and unlettered people who crowded to their sermons.

6

THE FRIARS IN SOCIETY

The setting up, in the thirteenth century, of the orders of friars—Dominican, Franciscan, Augustinian and Carmelite—created something of a crisis for the Church. Up till then there had been two types of ministry—regular and secular. The 'regulars' were the monks, nuns and canons of the various orders. These were men and women who had entered a religious house or monastery and had taken vows to remain there for the rest of their lives, and to cut themselves off from the life of the world while they devoted themselves to liturgical, scholastic and other kinds of work. Their main task was to perform what was called the *Opus Dei* which meant attendance at a daily course of services which occurred roughly at three-hourly intervals. But they had, of course, many other things to do. They had to look after the community and see that its members were properly clothed and fed. They had novices to train and old monks to nurse. They had extensive buildings to keep in good repair, and, as time went on, large estates to manage. But each monastery was a self-contained unit. The responsibilities of its members lay within the community and not with the world outside. Although some of the Austin canons did some pastoral work and acted as parish priests, this was exceptional. The members of the religious orders lived their own lives, separated from the world, and enclosed within the high walls of their monasteries.

The 'secular' clergy were the parish priests, of whom there were many kinds. A few of the men in holy orders were members of the noble families, but many of these took little interest in the parishes from which they drew their incomes. Some of them held a large number of benefices in plurality; appointed other men to look after their parishes; and lived at court where they did the work now done by the civil service. The men who did the actual work in the parishes were often of humble origin, local men who had received little education or training for their work. The good, conscientious men did their best. They visited their parishioners in their homes, they gave them absolution and spiritual comfort, they taught them the faith and they administered the sacraments.

Then, quite suddenly, there burst upon the world a new type of ministry—the friar. He was a 'regular', for he took vows to observe a Rule, wore a distinctive habit, and belonged to a community. But he was not cut off from the world like the monk. Far from it, for it was his special work to go among people and minister to them, not only to the sick and poor but wherever he could get an entrance. He was a preacher and evangelist, who did his utmost to attract people to his sermons. He believed that the Order to which he belonged had been raised up by God to reform the Church and to make up the deficiencies among the parochial clergy.

The appearance of the friars obviously created a very real problem for the parish priest. Before their appearance he had no rivals. The monks did not interfere with him in any way since they seldom emerged from their monasteries. But the friars seemed to be usurping some of the ancient and inalienable rights of the parish priest. They were certainly acting as spiritual guides to many of the laity. They were undoubtedly enticing people away from the parish churches on Sunday mornings. And in doing all this they clearly had the support of the highest authorities in the Church. It was no wonder that the parish clergy began to wonder what was happening.

Imagine, for example, a town like Beverley in York-shire where the church life revolved round the Minister which was the joy and pride of the borough. Presiding over the other buildings of the town in its dignity and grandeur, the Minster and its clergy provided all the spiritual food that man could need. It was adminitered by a provost and a number of prebendaries, vicars choral and what were called 'clerks of the barfel'. If they had all been there this number of clergy would have been impressive; but most of the prebendaries were pluralists and absentees, and many of the clerks were studying at one of the universities. But there would probably be normally about fifteen clergy serving the Minster and the other churches in the town. But, about the year 1250, the friars arrived, first Dominicans and then Franciscans. Within a few years each had built a monas-tery in, or close to, the town, and the friars were using it as a base for pastoral work among the people. In 1304 each house contained 38 friars, a total of 76, thus out-numbering the parochial clergy by about five to one. Among these friars were a good many well-educated and able men, good preachers with some knowledge of the world, pleasant people to have in your home or to listen to on a Sunday morning. It was no wonder that the local clergy became anxious. Nor were they much encouraged when they discovered that the bishops were being told by the pope that they were to give these new-comers all the help which they could.

St. Francis had seen this danger right from the start of his Order, and had made it clear that the friars, who were committed to a life of humility as well as of poverty, should not try to force themselves where they were not wanted or attempt to interfere with the rights of the clergy. In the Rule which he wrote he declared that 'the friars are forbidden to preach in any diocese if the bishop objects to it', and in his last Will and Testament he said: 'If I were as wise as Solomon, and met the poorest priests of the world, I would still refuse to preach against their will in the parish in which they live'. No doubt the early friars did their best to observe the principles which St. Francis had given them. So long as they were homeless evangelists, it did not matter much where they delivered their message. If they were not allowed to preach or to minister to the people in one place they could always go off and do so somewhere else. But when they became more stable and built their own churches and friaries in most of the major cities in Europe, the problem became very acute.

The papacy generally supported the friars. Most popes were aware of the fact that the Church was very much in need of reform, and had hopes that the members of the new Orders would bring this about. Many of them saw that there would be trouble, and that the friars would therefore need a good deal of support, and they issued bulls and sent letters to the bishops telling them what to do. St. Francis had hated the idea of his friars receiving any privileges. 'In virtue of obedience', he wrote 'I strictly forbid the firars, wherever they may be, to petition the Roman Curia, either personally or through an intermediary, for a papal brief, whether it concerns a church or any other place, or even in order to preach, or because they are being persecuted'. But from 1231 onwards privileges were heaped upon them.

The tension between the friars and the parochial clergy generally turned on three things—the right to preach, to hear confessions and to bury the dead. All were perfectly good things which would be more or less taken for granted today. But things were very different in the Middle Ages. The friars certainly attracted people to their sermons and to their worship; but, by so doing, they drew them away from their parish churches, and it is not surprising that some of the clergy felt aggrieved when they found on a Sunday morning that half their flock had gone off to the Franciscan church to take part in a Mass sung by thirty young friars and to hear a sermon by a man who had just arrived from the South of France, full of information and charm. Again, the friars became very popular as confessors. This may have been due to the fact that they were well-trained spiritual guides; but it may also have been because it is less of an ordeal to make your confession to a stranger than to your own parish priest. Moreover, the friars soon got the reputation rightly or wrongly, of giving absolution very readily, especially if the penitent promised a gift to the community. Or again, the friars were often so greatly respected that many people wanted to be buried in their churches and graveyards, believing that this would be of advantage to them on the Day of Judgement.

One can sympathise with the clergy. It was bad enough to feel that you were losing your hold on your people. It was worse when money which should have come into your pocket began finding its way into the coffers of the friars.

So far as the preaching was concerned there was very little that could be done about it. The parochial clergy were, for the most part, incapable of doing much in the way of preaching. It was not generally regarded as very important, and few of the clergy had any training for it. But many of the bishops were urging the clergy to give more instruction and exhortation to their people, and could hardly blame the friars for fulfilling their hopes.

The problem of the friars hearing confession was more

difficult because a legal problem was involved. According to Canon Law it was the duty of everyone to confess all his sins once a year to his parish priest. This annual, spiritual spring-cleaning played a very important part in the relationship between a priest and a member of his flock, and was not lightly to be discarded. If lay people were to go and confess their sins to a friar they were really wasting their time, as the same sins would have to be confessed all over again when they went to the rector, if the law was to be observed.

The problem of burials was made more difficult because of burial fees. If the friars accepted a person for burial in their church or cemetery they expected to collect the customary fee and often suggested, or demanded, substantial legacies as well.

This sort of thing was disastrous for the clergy, whose livelihood depended upon fees and gifts of this kind. But the friars soon acquired, in some places, a bad reputation for trying to get hold of burial rights. As one of the chroniclers said: 'they hang round the corpses of wealthy men like dogs round carrion, each waiting greedily for his portion'.

The coming of the friars did, then, create a number of difficulties, as the parish priest stood to lose his Sunday congregation, his Easter heart-to-heart with his parishoners, and even perhaps a considerable part of his income.

Problems of this kind were cropping up all over Europe, and, in some places, they were more serious than in England. But here in England there were some ugly incidents. At Worcester, for example, on 1st March 1290, a man called Henry Poche died. As soon as this happened, the Franciscans said that he had left instructions that he wished to be buried in their churchyard. But when the monks at the Cathedral heard this, they thought that they had a claim on him, and the Sacrist seized the corpse and carried it off to their premises. The Franciscans, robbed of their prey, appealed to Archbishop Pecham (who was himself a Franciscan) for support The Archbishop thereupon wrote to the Bishop of Worcester ordering him to see that the body of Henry Poche was returned to the friars. The Bishop carried out various investigations, at the end of which he declared that the deceased had undoubtedly expressed a desire to be buried by the monks and not by the friars, and refused to carry out the Archbishop's instructions. Pecham continued to support his own Order, and sometime in December the body was stolen by the Franciscans who carried it away in triumph to their friary—though in what state it now was, eight months after the poor man's death, is not revealed. Ten years or so later a similar dispute occurred between the Dominicans and the Canons of Exeter over the body of Sir Henry Ralegh which was bandied about for some time 'by meanes whereof the said corps lay so longe unburied that it stanke'.

Disputes of this kind did the Church no good; and, so serious were matters becoming, that, in 1300, Boniface VIII issued regulations to try to settle the tensions which existed between the friars and the other clergy. His rules were that the friars might preach in their own churches or in public places except at certain times; that only certain friars, chosen by themselves and licensed by the bishops, might hear confessions; and that if friars buried people in their churches or churchyards one quarter of all fees and legacies should be given to the parish priest. Attempts were made to see that these sensible rules were observed, and the registers of English bishops in the fourteenth century contain lists of friars who were licensed as confessors. The bishops were, for the most part, very careful, and gave their licences only sparingly. Of the fourteen friars chosen out of the community at Bedford only four were accepted; and again only four of the twenty-four recommended by the guardian of Oxford, though two more were afterwards added on the grounds that they were doctors of divinity.

Boniface's attempt to provide a solution of the problems helped to calm things down a little; but complaints against the friars continued from church leaders and others. The first great critic of the friars was Richard Fitzralph who was born in Ireland about 1300, and became, in due course, Archbishop of Armagh. Fitzralph had seen something of the Franciscan friars at Dundalk where he was brought up, and had been favourably impressed by them. But, as time went on, he became more and more disturbed by their behaviour. His chief criticism was of their standard of living. They called themselves 'Friars Minor' and were supposed to be humble, to live austerely, and to be devoted to the service of the poor. Yet he found them busily collecting privileges from the pope, usurping the rights of the parochial clergy, getting money by means both fair and foul, and building themselves commodious and comfortable monasteries. All this seemed to him to be a denial of what they stood for, and he was determined to expose them as hypocrites.

In 1356 he used the occasion of a series of popular sermons, which he had been asked to give to the people of London, to attack the friars for their interference in the rights of the clergy and for the luxury of their lives. In the following year, when he was at Avignon, conducting various legal disputes with the Archbishop of Canterbury and others, he again attacked the friars for hearing confessions and giving easy absolution, often on receipt

of a bribe. He also complained that the friars were 'stealing children' by which he meant that they enticed young
boys into the Order against the wishes of their parents
and before they were old enough to know their own
minds. Fitzralph was a serious critic who thought that
certain abuses needed to be reformed. He was neither
violent nor abusive, but he complained bitterly that all
discipline was being undermined by men who would do
almost anything to get money. Naturally the friars spoke
up for themselves, two English Franciscans, Roger Con-
way and William Woodford, trying to defend the friars'
actions.

John Wyclif, like Richard Fitzralph, was at first a
supporter of the friars, but, later in life, he became one
of their more formidable critics. His first assault was on
their interpretation of the meaning of the Eucharist, but
he went on from this to attack other things which they
were teaching, especially about the poverty of Christ
and about the validity of Masses and Letters of Fraternity to gain salvation. All this he thought unhealthy, and
it was not long before he began to criticise the whole way
of life of the friars. He accused them of destroying the
age-old relationship between the parish priest and his
flock, of thinking far too much about money and using
many improper means of making themselves rich, of
'stealing children', and even of immorality. He thought
all the four Orders guilty of these things, but he chose
the Franciscans for his special condemnation because of
the high standards set by St. Francis and of what he regarded as the treachery and hypocrisy of his followers.
They pretend, he said, to be poor when, in fact, they
live extremely well; they boast that they never touch
money when in fact they are handling it all the time,
though with gloves on.

70

Wyclif became so bitter and intolerant in his later years that he would have liked to have the friars expelled. He came to regard them as papal spies, bishops' agents, a poison in the life of the Church which ought to be removed. Whatever good they may have done in the early days was long since lost by their atrocious behaviour, and the sooner they were got rid of the better.

If we turn from the theologians to the poets we find the same sort of thing. William Langland complained of the greed and cupidity of the friars who are corrupted by their love of money. Langland was a man of high ideals who was grieved at what he thought was a terrible downfall, where men who should have set an example of poverty and humility were, in fact, avaricious and boastful.

Langland's attitude towards the friars was taken up by many other writers in the fourteenth century. The friars in Chaucer's *Canterbury Tales* are despicable men— rapacious, immoral, undisciplined, deceitful and hypocritical. Of the friar who joined the party going to Canterbury he says:

'For he had power of confessioun,
As sayde him-self, more than a curat,
For of his Ordre he was licenciat.
Ful swetely herde he confessioun,
And plesaunt was his absolucioun;
He was an esy man to yeve penaunce
Ther as he wiste to have a good pitaunce'—

by which he means that the friar, having managed to get the bishop's licence to hear confessions, was always willing to give absolution and a light penance if the penitent were prepared to give a good sum of money to the friars. The Wife of Bath hints at the immorality of the friars when she blandly remarks that since the fairies had been got rid of, women have now nothing to fear on their travels except a chance meeting with a friar.

The political songs which were written in the fourteenth century also contain a great many criticisms of the friars. One says that, if a rich man dies, the friars are round in no time; but that if a poor man dies, and his relations call on the friars to ask if he can be buried in their church-yard, they are told that the guardian is away at the moment. Another says that the friars find out when a married man is going to be away from home for some time and then seduce his wife. Another, describing a pageant in which a Franciscan appeared in a fiery chariot, cried out 'Brent be thai alle'.

And so it went on, the friars being accused of sexual immorality, cupidity, insincerity, hypocrisy, and most other vices. These criticisms were directed to the friars of all Orders, but the Franciscans got the hardest knocks. People were aware of what St. Francis had done. They knew both the Rule and the Testament, and they felt that the friars of their generation had betrayed their founder's wishes and broken their own vows.

> 'Why hold ye not Saint Francis rule and testament
> Sith Francis saith that God shewed him this living
> and this rule?'

asks Jack Upland; and it was not easy for the friars to defend themselves, though some, like Daw Topias, attempted to do so. Topias, though describing himself as being 'as lewid as a leke', not only puts up some sort of defence, but also carries the war into the enemies' camp and has a good crack at what he called 'that wickid worme, Wiclyf be his name'.

It is, of course, true that the standard of life of the

friars in the year 1400 was different from what it had been nearly two centuries earlier. It is also true that out of some 1,500 Franciscan friars in England some would not be living up to the ideals set by St. Francis. But how far the criticisms of the period were justified it is hard to say. Friar-baiting had obviously become a popular game in the literary world, and some of the writers may have had very little first-hand knowledge of the sins and wickednesses which they so much enjoyed attacking.

The two most serious criticisms were that the friars were interfering with the work of the parochial clergy and that they were far too much concerned with raising money. To the first of these the friars could reply that they were commissioned by the pope to preach, and that if, by doing so, they won the respect and friendship of people they must be allowed to give them spiritual help by hearing their confessions, praying for them and allowing them to be buried in the friars' cemeteries. If the parochial clergy were not giving the people what they needed, then they should improve their techniques.

To the charge of luxury and avarice the friars had no simple or straightforward reply. In the early days, when there were only a few of them, they had managed to live very simply in huts and hovels and even in disused churches and caves. But with the rapid growth of the Order, and the advance in learning, something better than this had to be provided for them. From what we know of the English Franciscan houses none of them could be called luxurious, though many of them had large and well-appointed churches in which to gather together their congregations. So far as their domestic buildings were concerned, these were mostly fairly modest owing to the fact that space was so limited. The old monasteries, each of which contained, on average, about 12 choir-monks, were far more spacious and impressive than the friaries which, although they housed, on average, about 17 brethren, were often tucked away in the towns on very modest sites. The monasteries, moreover, owned very considerable estates from which they got their food, and, on the rents of which they could afford to employ large numbers of servants to look after them, and to build up large libraries and great stores of plate and vestments. The fourteenth century friars may have looked very different from those who came to England in 1224, but their standard of living was still far below that of other 'religious'.

It was unusual, though not unknown, for a friary to own property from which rents could be collected. This meant that, for the most part, the friars in England had to collect from the public the money necessary to support about 3,000 men and women and to provide the things necessary for the work. It is probable that the friars were sometimes very much to blame for the methods which they used in getting the money which they needed; but there is plenty to show that people gave willingly for their support. A few friars were, no doubt, fairly well off, but this would be due to very exceptional circumstances. John (or Robert) Lambourne, who came from a noble family, joined the Franciscans early in the fourteenth century and became confessor to Queen Isabella, the wife of Edward III, in 1327. In later life he was awarded a state pension and assigned a 'decent chamber' in the London friary where he was to live with a companion of his own choice, a clerk and two servants. Another friar, called John Malberthorp, had a pension of 40 marks a year from the Exchequer—a large sum when it is remembered that the basic stipend for a vicar was five marks a year. A good many friars also had some sort of private income from gifts made by friends and well-wishers, as the wills show.

But for most of the friars life was fairly simple and austere. By the middle of the fourteenth century it was still customary for them to go without footwear or the author of *Pierce the Ploughman's Crede* would not have complained that he had seen some Franciscans going about in buckled shoes. It was still the custom for all the friars to sleep together in dormitories, or Wyclif would not have complained that doctors of divinity were demanding private cells. It is also interesting to note that a considerable number of friars in various countries left the Order about this time in order to join one of the better-endowed communities, generally on the excuse that they could not stand the poverty and simplicity of the Friars Minor. At least sixty-four Franciscan friars had permission to do this between 1335 and 1378, though none of these came from the province of England.

Some of the criticisms, coming soon after the Black Death, may have been due to the fact that the friars were passing through a very bad time. There is no doubt that the plague hit the friars very hard as they lived in the towns and were (we hope) helping to care for the sick and the dying. In some parts of Europe the friars were more or less wiped out, and though we have no evidence for England the mortality was undoubtedly very severe. Dublin and Drogheda in Ireland both lost half their members, and there is reason to believe that much the same happened in England, reducing the total number of Friars Minor from about 1,500 to 750. This presented the friars with a great problem. If the work was to go on, then new recruits must be found as quickly as possible. This probably meant that standards were lowered and that some young men were accepted who were not really suitable. The friars certainly took some who were well below the minimum age. Poor little Henry Wytbery at the age of ten was handed over to the friars by his father to make it impossible for him to inherit the family estates. Although Henry had no desire to become a friar, he was clothed in the habit and given the tonsure although still under eleven years of age. This must have been exceptional, but it does give some justification to the criticism that the friars were 'stealing children'. Similarly at the universities, to which boys came at the age of fourteen or less, the friars may well have done their utmost to persuade some of them to join the Order; and it is interesting to note that, before the plague, there were generally about 80 Franciscans at Oxford whereas in 1377 the number had gone up to 103.

But although the friars came in for a good deal of criticism and even abuse, the public as a whole seem to have supported them right up to the Dissolution. If legacies are anything to go by, there is clear evidence that people were glad to leave money to the friars. It is estimated that, of all known wills of Oxford citizens, one third contain bequests to the Friars Minor; and the same would be true of other places. This showed that people appreciated what the friars were doing and valued their services. It is also interesting to note that, in spite of the tensions which sometimes occurred between the friars and the parish priests, nearly half the known legacies to the Franciscans of Exeter came from the clergy.

We must not, therefore, take the bitter or mocking words of Wyclif and Chaucer too seriously. Not everyone thought as they did; and, indeed, Jack Straw, the peasants' leader in the rebellion of 1381, said that he would like to get rid not only of the monarchy but of all the monks and secular clergy, leaving only the friars who would suffice for celebrating the sacraments.

7

THE OBSERVANTS

England was only one of the thirty-four provinces into which the Order of Friars Minor was divided. Of these, fourteen were in Italy, six in Central Europe, five in France and three in Spain, while the rest covered territory which extended from Ireland to the Holy Land. There were also a number of 'vicariates' which brought in such places as Scotland, Russia and the Far East. In its early days the English province made a very considerable contribution to the history of the Order, since it provided two of the Ministers General and a large proportion of the leading scholars. But in later years, the province of England seems to have become rather isolated. It certainly went through none of the devastating controversies and disputes which disturbed the Order so much in the later Middle Ages and eventually led to its division into two.

We have already seen that, almost from the beginning, there were two parties and two policies among the friars. There were the intransigent 'Spirituals' who wanted to preserve the standards laid down by St. Francis, and there were the more progressive, co-operative 'Conventuals' who thought that their first duty was to be loyal to the Church and to let the Order be used as the authorities thought best. These two policies created much unhappiness and suffering in some parts of Europe; but there is no sign of them in England.

In addition to internal disputes, the Franciscans in some places also got embroiled in the long-drawn-out fight against heresy. A number of Friars Minor acted as inquisitors and a few were themselves tried for heresy, four of them actually being burnt to death in Marseilles in 1318 for having disagreed with the official interpretation of poverty as expressed in a series of papal declarations. But nothing like this happened in England. Except for Wyclif and his followers there was very little heresy in England, and no Inquisition. Some Franciscans took part in the various trials of Wyclif but so far as we know, none were themselves suspected of sharing his opinions. A friar called William Russel, who was Guardian of the London convent in 1425, preached, among other things, the theory that tithes need not be paid to the parish priest but could be given to any charitable purpose. This was understood to be an attempt to channel money out of the pockets of the clergy and into those of the friars, and Russell was charged with heresy by both universities. He fled to Rome, but shortly afterwards returned to England where he gave himself up, recanted and was set free. Some years later a friar called Isaac Cusack was degraded by his university for preaching heretical views about evangelical poverty. Another, John Mardisley, in the fourteenth century, criticised the doctrines put forward by Boniface VIII about the state being in subjection to the Church. But these were individual cases and of no great importance.

A few English Franciscans got themselves into serious trouble, but this was for political rather than religious reasons. Early in the fifteenth century a few friars were arrested and charged with having committed treason by trying to stir up opposition to Henry IV and by saying that Richard II was still alive and remained the true King of England. A Cambridge friar who had given his support to this idea was accused by a woman of being a traitor. The justices do not seem to have taken this as much more than a joke, as they ordered the friar to fight the woman though with one hand tied behind his back. The duel, in fact, never took place as the Archbishop of Canterbury stepped in and forbade this unseemly proposal. But some friars in the midlands did get into very great trouble, among them eight friars from Leicester, including Roger Frisby the guardian, who were tried for conspiring against the king by trying to get men to go and search for Richard II in Scotland and by inviting Owen Glendower to invade England from the west. These eight friars were all hanged at Tyburn in 1402.

Meanwhile, in other parts of the world, the Order was running into great difficulty. The members of the 'Spiritual' party (often known as *Fraticelli*), who claimed to be the only true followers of St. Francis, were hunted down and put in prison. The Church authorities had their own ideas as to how the Friars Minor should live, and were not going to be thwarted by bands of fanatics. Yet these men carried on their campaign for what they believed to be right, getting some support and sympathy from those who were critical of the relaxations, and what they regarded as deterioration, among the members of the party in power. About the middle of the fourteenth century small groups of friars were being formed, pledged to go back to the rough and exacting conditions of the early days by living in caves rather in comfortable convents, and by begging their bread instead of raising money.

In 1350 a friar called Gentile of Spoleto persuaded the authorities to give him four small hermitages in central Italy—one of them being the well-known Carceri on the hillside above Assisi—and to put small groups of friars into them to live a life of complete poverty. But, within a few years people were accusing them of heresy, and the experiment came to an end. But soon after this, in 1365,

Paul de'Trinci collected together a little community of like-minded friars in the remote hermitage of Brugliano, high up in the hills. The purpose of this experiment was to adopt the strictest possible interpretation of the Rule, however difficult and uncomfortable this might be. It was at this point that the Order entered on the path which led, 142 years later, to its being finally divided into two— Observants (as the stricter branch now came to be called) and Conventuals.

The reforming movement soon began to attract a good many enthusiastic men; and, before long, other hermitages were put at their disposal including two in the valley of Rieti—Greccio (the scene of Francis' Christmas crib) and Fonte Colombo (the place where the wrote the Rule). In 1415 they were also given the use of the Portiuncula where Francis's mission began and ended. From then onwards the Observant movement forged ahead, greatly helped by the holiness of life and marvellous preaching of men like St. Bernardino of Siena, St. John of Capistrano, St. James of the March and Albert of Sarteano, together described as 'the four pillars of the observance', The number of houses increased rapidly as new places were provided for them, or as existing convents decided to change over and adopt the stricter rules and standards of the Observants. The problem now was whether or not the Observants should be given more independence from the more steady-going Conventuals. Should they be allowed to choose their own leaders, to have their own provincial ministers, and to hold their own chapters and make their own constitutions? Again, how was all this going to affect the Clarisses and the members of the Third Order, many of whom expressed a wish to be associated with the Observants rather than remaining in the care and under the jurisdiction of the Conventuals?

The history of the Order in the fifteenth century is largely taken up with the question as to whether it could hold together as one, or whether it would have to be divided into two. There were some who hoped that the whole Order would carry out reforms so drastic that there would be no need for a stricter party among the friars. Others hoped that unity would be maintained by having a single form of government but allowing for local deviations, so that while some houses wanted to show their determination to reproduce, as far as possible, the standards of the early days, others would accept certain changes, even if they were of a relaxing nature, if it meant that the friars would thereby be of greater service to the Church. Attempts along these lines were made; but in the end it became clear that there would have to be division; and, in 1517, the Pope, Leo X, finally divided the Order into two, each with its own Minister General, its own customs, and its own jurisdiction.

While the Observant way of life was gaining ground rapidly in Italy, Spain and France, there is no sign of its arousing any interest in England. John Zouch, who was Provincial Minister in 1404, was a keen reformer who may have known what was going on in other countries and have hoped for a similar movement in England. But he got no support; and, to remove all source of danger, he was tactfully made Bishop of Llandaff in 1407.

Nothing happened during the next fifty years; but in 1454 the pious Henry VI wrote to the leader of the Observants, John of Capistrano, asking him if he would bring a party of friars of the strict observance to England. John replied that this was impossible as he was just starting off for Hungary to take part in the defence of Eastern Europe against the Moslem invasions. He suggested that Henry might approach the Observants in France; but nothing came of this, and it was not until 1482 that the Observants first set foot in England.

It is difficult to know for certain why, when the movement was so active in other countries, the English friars remained unmoved. Some historians think that the answer lies in the fact that the English friars, though relaxed in some ways, were a good deal less in need of reform than their brethern on the Continent. Whether this was so or not, the Franciscans in England continued to be popular among the people, inspite of the attacks of their critics. Gifts continued to pour into the convents right up to the end—gifts from all sorts of people, the king, monks, parish clergy, the nobility, tradesmen, even labourers. While most of the gifts were in money, many were in kind. Among the legacies given to the Franciscans in York we find a cup of black crystal, a large basin for washing the feet, gowns of cloth of gold and of silk, a gilt spoon and many other objects, some of considerable value. George Darrell, who made his will in 1433, expressed a wish to be buried in the friars' church at York and bequeathed 5 marks for masses to be said for a year. For every priest friar who attended his funeral he left 1s. and for every novice 6d. Also, for the common use of the friars, he left a green bed with white coverlets, a red and green counterpane, a pair of blankets, two pairs of linen sheets, two red curtains, a quilt, a mattress and six pewter vessels. What the friars did with all this stuff no one knows; and we are left wondering what St. Francis would have said if he had been present when all these things arrived.

A study of the wills of the fifteenth century shows us that the English friars were amassing a good deal of property and considerable financial resources; but it also reveals the fact that many people approved of them and valued their prayers as an aid to salvation. Even Latimer once said that, when he was going through a severe illness and thought that he might die, he was tempted to become a friar in the belief that this would help him to get into heaven more easily.

All this shows that the English friars of the fifteenth century had moved some way from the standards laid down by St. Francis, but there was no sign of a reforming movement among them, and the Observant ideal seems completely to have passed them by. When, therefore, the Observants were eventually introduced into England it was not because the English friars wanted help in reaching a higher standard, nor yet because the English people were anxious for a better type of Franciscan. It was due to the fact that Edward IV wanted, near to his palace in Greenwich, a community of God-fearing and selfsacrificing men who would pray for his soul.

It was towards the end of 1480 that Edward sent for the Vicar General of the Observants living north of the Alps, and told him that he would like to establish a house of Observants at Greenwich. In so doing the King may have been influenced by his sister, Margaret of Burgundy, whose father-in-law had done much for the Observants in France. The Vicar General, a Breton called William Bertho, said that he could do nothing without the consent of the pope, but there was no difficulty there, and the pope, Sixtus IV, himself a Franciscan (though not Observant), gave permission for the erection of a church, a cloister and the necessary domestic buildings for the use of the Observants of Greenwich.

As there were no Observant friars in England a party had to be made up from somewhere on the mainland of Europe; and, in 1482, about twelve friars, mostly from the Low Countries and under the leadership of Bernard of Lochen, arrived in England.

The convent which was being prepared for them was not yet built, but there were some buildings on the site which the friars used until the friary was ready for them. The house was put under the jurisdiction of the Observant province of Cologne, and remained so until 1499 when it was thought expedient to found an English province of the Observance with power to hold chapters and elect its own Provincial Vicar.

By this time there were four Observant houses in England, for the pope, on the advice of King Henry VII, had asked the Archbishop of Canterbury and the Bishops of Durham and Ely to choose five of the existing Franciscan houses, especially those in which the friars 'lived a reprobate life', to see that the friars living in them were removed to other friaries, and to hand over the buildings to the Observants. It looks as if the prelates may have found some difficulty in carrying out the pope's instructions, perhaps because very few of the friaries could be classed as 'reprobate', or because it was impossible to get the friars to go away. In the end they managed to get three houses which could be transferred—Newcastle-on-Tyne, where plans had already been made to change over the Observant obedience, Southampton, where things may have been somewhat lax, and Canterbury, though here we have some evidence of a flourishing and reasonably conscientious community.

Then, about 1500, Henry decided to found a new friary for Observants at Richmond, near to another royal palace of Sheen, and seven years later, a new house for Observants was founded at Newark. A proposal to set up a house at Wakefield about twenty years later came to nothing. This meant that, by 1507, there were six houses of Observants in England, and that was all. The first occupants of these houses seem to have been almost entirely foreigners, mostly from Belgium and Holland; but naturally it was not long before Englishmen asked to be admitted. By 1491 English names were beginning to appear among the friars of Greenwich—Thomas Garnett, William Elliott and Richard Morcrofte. John Forest (who was later put to death) is thought to have entered the Order, probably at Greenwich, about the same year. Hugh Rich, another martyr, was at Greenwich when ordained acolyte in 1517 and at Newark when ordained priest two years later. There is not much doubt, therefore, that the six Observant houses filled up fairly quickly, though there is no clear evidence of any existing friars wanting to change their allegiance and join the Observants.

In the thirty years between 1491 and 1521 the registers of the Bishops of London record the ordinations of 107 Observant friars, mostly from Greenwich and Richmond; and most of these were Englishmen. It needed foreign friars to start the Observant movement in England, but, once it got established, it quickly attracted a number of zealous and courageous men, some of whom were content to lay down their lives rather than compromise their faith.

8

THE DISSOLUTION

The founding of the six Observant houses brought the
number of Franciscan friaries in England to sixty. Most
of these had been in existence since the thirteenth century, and none for less than 100 years. During the 300
years of their existence no house had come to an end
through mismanagement or lack of support. The friars
were, therefore, a part of the English scene, well-known
as they travelled about the country, and, for the most
part, well-liked. The number of friars had gone down
considerably at the time of the Black Death in the fourteenth century; but they had gradually risen since then
and, by the beginning of the sixteenth century, there
were probably about a thousand Franciscan friars in
England.

But some of the friaries were, by now, in rather a bad
way. The friars had been unable, for some time, to spend
much money on their buildings or on their other possessions. In some places they had had to sell some of their
goods. Some had dug up their waterpipes in order to sell
the lead. A good many had let their gardens to laymen,
or had allowed outsiders to come and live in part of
their monastery. At Reading, for example, three sets of
rooms had been fitted up as apartments, one being given
to the Guardian, and the other two being let to lay
people, a servant of the King and a Lady St. John. Most
of the friaries made a little money by putting up guests,
some of them for a long period.

Not only were the buildings looking the worse for
wear, the same might be said of the communities. In

some ways the fire had gone out of the movement, except among the Observants. Those who were now attached to the Order were living on the past, content to lead a fairly easy-going life without much imagination or enthusiasm. Though there are some hints of misbehaviour when the visitations took place, it is doubtful if there was much that was seriously wrong. There was some slackness, and there were some flagrant breaches of the vow of poverty; but the Order was still attracting young men, as is shown by the Ordination lists; for the Archbishop of York ordained a number of friars, one of them as sub-deacon, in February 1538, only a few months before the dissolution. In spite, therefore, of the zeal and self-sacrifice of the Observants, the other houses went on much as before, and, so far as is known, no member of any of the 54 existing houses left in order to join the stricter regime of the Observants.

So far as scholarship is concerned, the great days of the Order had long since gone. The universities were now very much on their feet, and, although the friars' schools continued, they did not turn out any very distinguished men. A good many friars still came to the houses at Oxford and Cambridge, and took their degrees but this did not lead to much output. Richard Brinkley was perhaps the most learned Franciscan friar of his generation. He was a doctor of divinity of both Oxford and Cambridge, and a student of Greek and Hebrew; but he is not known to have written anything of importance. Another friar, Henry Standish, was also a learned man; but he soon became involved in controversial and political affairs, through which he steered his course in such a way as to serve his own ends. He began as a conservative catholic and staunch opponent of the new ideas now coming in from Germany. He took part in the trial of

'Little Bilney' in 1527, and was, for a time, a close friend of Katharine of Aragon; yet in the end he accepted the royal supremacy without hesitation, being, by then, Bishop of St. Asaph. He died in 1535 leaving £40 to pay for his funeral and £43 for a decent memorial to be erected in the Greyfriars Church in London.

Cranmer once praised the community of Franciscan friars in Cambridge, which, he said, contained a number of learned men; but he was, perhaps, referring to the fact that among the Cambridge friars there were some who were supporting the new theology which was being hotly debated in the university in the sixteenth century. We know that, in the 1520s, the works of Luther were being smuggled into England, and that students in the universities were reading and discussing them. There was certainly a good deal of debate going on in Cambridge, possibly due to the fact that books were being distributed in East Anglia by merchants and others who had contacts with the Low Countries. But, in our records of the conversations which took place in the White Horse Tavern, there is no mention of a Franciscan. There were however, friars at Cambridge like John Cardmaker who became a passionate reformer and gave his life for his convictions in 1555. Another, called William Roy, left Cambridge to join William Tyndale at Hamburg in 1524 and was eventually burnt to death as a heretic in Portugal. Among the reforming party at Oxford was an Italian friar called Nicholas de Burgo who strongly advocated the King's divorce and became a royal favourite. Another friar, called John Joseph, who was at Oxford from about 1520 onwards, became one of Cranmer's chaplains and Rector of St. Mary le Bow in London.

In the theological discussions which were now taking place the friars were very much divided. Some accepted with alacrity and enthusiasm the new ideas which were being circulated, seeing in them hope for a radical reform of the Church and for progress towards the City of God. But there were many others who were frightened of change, who looked back to the 'good old days', and who were alarmed by the new theology which threatened to overthrow the world in which they lived. There can be little doubt that some pretty hot debates took place in some of the convents between conservative and progressive members of the community.

About this time, in the 1520s, Wolsey was beginning to formulate plans for reforming all the religious houses in England and of closing down those which refused to be reformed, possibly with a view to raising some money for his educational and academic projects. As far as the friars were concerned, he was not much interested in them as they were too poor to be able to provide much for his plans. He was, however, suspicious of the Observants, who had close contacts with the papacy and might, in the end, cause trouble. But, although Wolsey closed down 29 religious houses between 1524 and 1529, no Franciscan friary was affected.

By now, however, the question of the King's marriage was beginning to be discussed, and, within the next ten years, not only would the church in England find itself completely separated from the Church of Rome, but all the 'religious'—monks, canons, friars and nuns—were to disappear altogether from the English scene. In the debate on the validity of Henry's marriage to Katharine of Aragon and on the rights and wrongs of his defying the pope and tearing the Church in England away from the papal obedience, the Franciscan friars, with the exception of the Observants, seemed strangely indifferent, and were, apparently quite content first to accept the royal supremacy and then to allow their communities to be dispersed and their homes emptied and despoiled.

The friars were, no doubt, divided in their opinions and emotions; but most of them did what the rest of the country did, which was to accept the new situation and make the best they could of it. Some went abroad, some left their convents and got whatever jobs they could, but a few felt that they must put up some sort of struggle against what they regarded as blasphemy and tyranny, even if they had to suffer for it. The first to lose their lives for conscience sake were two Observants, Richard Risby, Guardian of Canterbury, and Hugh Rich, Guardian of Richmond. Both of these men supported the cause of Elizabeth Barton, the Maid of Kent and both were executed together with the Maid at Tyburn on 21 April, 1534.

The King was now demanding that all clergy must take the Oath of Supremacy which acknowledged all that Henry had done and repudiated the authority of the papacy. He started with the friars because he regarded them as potentially dangerous. They were popular preachers; they moved about among the people; they had contacts with the Church in southern Europe and with the papacy; they were outside the control of the bishops; and some of them were known to be hot-headed men who were prepared to challenge what Henry was doing. Thomas Cromwell was, therefore, charged with drawing up a set of articles which were to be presented to the friars and to which each individual friar must give his assent. The articles included acceptance of Anne as queen and her children as the rightful heirs to the throne, acknowledgement of the King as 'supreme head of the English Church', repudiation of all papal authority in England, and a promise to preach these doctrines on every possible occasion. As it was thought that the Observants were the most likely to put up any resistance they were given a new Vicar Provincial, not a member of their Order but an Augustinian friar who was to visit them in their houses.

A visitation of the friaries now took place, and as the King had anticipated, it was the Observants who refused to accept the articles and were prepared to face the consequences. This was a blow the Henry who had always looked upon the Observants with favour. He often attended their church at Greenwich and had seen a good deal of them from time to time. When his daughter Elizabeth was born she was christened in the same church. Henry had always treated them with respect as a body of keen, enthusiastic, self-sacrificing men who could do much to strengthen and reform the Church. But in the matter of his policies Henry looked upon them with considerable suspicion. As early as 1532 William Peto, while preaching before the King at Greenwich, had publicly criticised his behaviour and rebuked him in the presence of his courtiers. Henry seems to have taken this fairly calmly and allowed Peto to go abroad for a bit. When he returned, he and Henry Elston were imprisoned for a short time, but again were allowed to go overseas where they lay low until the accession of Mary in 1553. Peto who had always supported Katharine and her daughter, Mary, then rose to high favour and was offered the bishopric of Salisbury in 1557.

Meanwhile a more dangerous opponent of the King had come to light in the person of John Forest who became Guardian of the Observants at Greenwich about 1532. Forest was a determined and courageous man who was prepared to give his life for what he felt to be right; and, as he went about stirring up opposition, Thomas

Cromwell provided himself with two spies, one called John Lawrence and the other Richard Lyst, who sent in reports of what Forest was saying and doing. Lyst had been out with Forest when he was preaching and he told Cromwell that he had often 'sytten undyr the pulpyt wyth a payre of redde earys', so ashamed was he of what was being said. In 1533 Forest was sent to one of the northern houses, but in the following year he found himself in the Tower. In 1536 he was living with the friars in London but two years later he was in prison again, charged with heresy. After a certain amount of inconstancy he eventually made his stand and was burnt to death on 22 May 1538 after having to listen to an inordinately long sermon by Latimer.

By now the Observants as a whole were being rounded up. In 1534 'two cartloads of friars' were carried to the Tower. Others were sent to other Franciscan houses where they were chained together and kept in confinement. Some fled to Scotland or overseas. One or two became members of another Order. Many of them died either from exhaustion or from violence. Anthony Brockby (sometimes known as Brown or Brorbe), a competent theologian formerly of Magdalen College, Oxford, was strangled with his own cord. Thomas Cortt and Thomas Belchian both died of starvation in prison. By 1537 the Observants as a body had more or less ceased to exist in England and their main convent, at Greenwich, had been handed over to the Conventuals.

While the Observant friars were being harried in this way, the King was planning the suppression of all monastic houses in his realm. He had begun this in 1534 with an order that a general survey of all ecclesiastical revenues should be made. In the following year Cromwell appointed Dr. Legh and Dr. Layton to visit and report on all the smaller religious houses, and in 1536 no less than 376 of the smaller houses went out of existence. This first act of suppression did not affect the friaries. Henry was out for money, and the friars, who had no estates to speak of, were clearly unable to contribute anything much. But, though poor, the friars could be a nuisance, as Henry had learned in his dealings with the Observants.

So, in 1538, Richard Ingworth, Bishop of Dover and previously Provincial Prior of the Dominican friars in England, was given orders to visit the friaries. Ingworth was, on the whole, a kind man who wanted to help the friars get out with as little fuss as possible. He himself had lost all interest in the religious life, and he expected others to feel the same. Within the next few months he visited, with the assistance of Dr. John London, all the friaries in England and Wales; made inventories of what he found there; persuaded the friars to hand everything over to him; and told them that they must go. He was very careful to tell them, on arrival, that he had come not to suppress their community but to reform it. If they were willing to be reformed the King would let them continue; otherwise they would have to go. So frightened and dispirited were the friars by this time that they all obediently went.

Ingworth's inventories show that all the communities were poor; that their property was in bad repair; that many of them had already got rid of some of their posessions in order to pay their debts; in fact, that gloom and despondency had settled upon them. At Gloucester the visitors had to sell the bees, corn, onions and apples in order to pay the wages of the servants whom the friars employed. At Coventry, although the roof of the Church was sound, the timber of the housing was 'stark nought'. At Bridgnorth the friars said that they had received in alms no more than 10s. in a whole year. At Lichfield they were in debt to the Bishop and others. A few places such as Bridgwater, had a fair amount of stuff—a table of alabaster with nine images, two goodly candlesticks and a pair of organs, twenty-one copes and 358 oz. of jewels and plate, but this was unusual.

Ingworth was genuinely worried about the future of the friars, who were being so obedient and helpful. He constantly wrote to Cromwell asking him to be good to the friars and give them their 'capacities'—that is, dispensation to get other work in the Church. In a letter of 10 March, 1538, he ends: 'besechyng yower lordschyp to be goode lorde for the pore ffreyrs capacytes; they be very pore and can have lytyll serves withowtt ther capacytes. The byschoyppys and curettes be very hard to them withowtt they have ther capacytes'. Nevertheless they had to go, even though they sometimes had people to plead for them. In a letter to Latimer, Ingworth tells how in some places the friars have 'many favourers and how great labour is made for their continuance. Divers', he said, 'trust to see them set up again, and some have gone up to sue for them'. But no help came. Henry was determined to get rid of them, and, by and large, the friars seemed ready to sign the deeds of surrender without demur. Occasionally they were humiliated and insulted by being forced to make a self-condemnatory statement, as happened at Aylesbury where the friars had to confess that they 'do profoundly consider that the perfection of a Christian living doth not consist in dumb ceremonies, wearing of a grey coat, disguising oneself after strange fashions, ducking and becking, in girding ourselves with a girdle full of knots, and other like papistical ceremonies, wherein we have been most principally practised and misled in times past'. But this was, perhaps, unusual.

So within a year or so the whole network of Franciscan houses in England came to an end and their occupants were turned out upon the world. As soon as it was known that they were going, various people tried to get hold of their buildings. At Reading, the townsfold tried to seize the friars' church in order to turn it into a Town Hall. At Bristol, the mayor and corporation pleaded for the stones of the Greyfriars' convent in order to repair the town walls and to build a wharf. At Cambridge, the University applied for possession of the friars' church in order to use it for academic purposes. In several places the town tried to get the conduit. At London, the friars' house was turned into Christ's Hospital, a school for boys. At Carmarthen, the mayor and aldermen wanted the friary for a grammar school.

At the time of the dissolution there were known to be about 600 Franciscan friars in England. Some were old men who had lived for many years in their convents, others were young men who had only recently joined them. In some ways they were better prepared for secular life than were the monks and canons, for they knew more of the world outside the cloister and had many useful contacts. But it was obviously going to be very difficult for them to find work. So far as we know, few, if any, went abroad to continue their life as sons of Francis in some more settled place. A few of the senior men got pensions, and most of the others got a small gift of some sort to keep them for a bit. Quite a number of those in Holy Orders are known to have got benefices, curacies or canonries. Of the seven friars who signed the deed of surrender at Chichester at least three got livings in the neighbourhood. Gilbert Berkeley, who was at York at the dissolution, had a somewhat adventurous career and spent some years in exile before becoming

Bishop of Bath and Wells in 1560. The only people who, after being turned out of their houses, tried to continue their way of life elsewhere were the Minoresses of Denney, some of whom went to a country house in Warwickshire where they did their best to keep the Rule and live the monastic life. Otherwise the whole Franciscan community which, in its palmiest days, had numbered over 1,700 members, quietly disappeared from the English scene, leaving little behind it except a few fragmentary remains, as at Chichester, Lynn and Richmond, to show what, at one time, had been a noble and vigorous element in the spiritual life of the country.

9

THE MODERN FRANCISCAN

With the dissolution of the friaries and the dispersal of their occupants it looked as if the Franciscan movement in England had come to an end. But this was not so; and when Queen Mary restored the doctrines and customs of the Roman Catholic Church in 1553 a group of Observant friars still living in Greenwich got together and re-opened the friary there. Peto and Elston now returned from abroad and a number of Spanish friars joined them. Reginald Pole, already appointed Archbishop of Canterbury was ordained priest in their church on 20th March, 1556, and was consecrated bishop there two days later.

But it was not to last for long. In 1558 Pole and the Queen both died, and the short-lived Catholic revival came to an abrupt end. Most of the friars then fled to the Netherlands or to Rome, but a few remained in hiding, carrying on their work in conditions of great danger and discomfort. As the anti-Roman fever increased after the excommunication of Queen Elizabeth and the launching of the Armada no doubt some were imprisoned, and at least one—John Jones (or Buckley) was put to death. But before he died he managed to hand on the seal of the Franciscan Province to William Staney who gave it to a friar called John Gennings early in the seventeenth century.

It was now clear that if the English province was to be re-established it would have to be based on foreign soil, and Gennings set up a friary at Gravelines, though shortly afterwards he moved it to Douai where there was already an English College. In 1618 the General

Chapter, meeting at Salamanca agreed to recognise an English province. Gennings acquired a house where the Franciscan Rule could be observed, and novices be received, trained and professed, so that the work in England might be pursued, even though it would have to be done secretly and in the face of great danger.

All the work of the Friars Minor in England was, for many years, organised from Douai. From here selected men were sent to England to give spiritual help to those who had not accepted the Elizabethan Settlement and to make converts of those who had. The friars who came knew the risks which they were running; but had not St. Francis run risks when he ventured into the territory of the Saracen armies in Egypt in the hopes of converting the Sultan to the Christian faith? In fact there was little persecution of Catholics during the reigns of James I (1603–1625) and Charles I (1625–1649) both of whom did their best to exercise tolerance. Charles' Roman Catholic wife, Henrietta Maria, insisted on bringing over a household which included one bishop and twenty-seven priests. Some Observant friars, mostly Spanish, became established in Somerset House, and the English friars found this a pleasant refuge in times of difficulty. But this period of comparative peace and security did not last very long; and when the Civil War broke out the net began to be drawn much tighter, and at least three friars of the English province lost their lives. The first of these was Thomas Bullaker who came not from Douai but from Spain. He worked for twelve years in London but was eventually arrested while saying Mass and was put to death on 12th October 1642. Henry Heath, a graduate of Cambridge, was a convert who joined the friars at Douai. He was sent to England early in 1643, but was taken prisoner as he walked from

Dover to London and was hanged. Arthur (or Francis) Bell joined the Order in Spain and later became Guardian at Douai where he lectured in Hebrew. After an attempt to restore the Order in Scotland he moved into England where he worked for six years. He was hanged on 11th December, 1643.

After the Restoration in 1660 things became much easier for the missionaries. Charles II was naturally sympathetic to Roman Catholics, and his brother, James II more so. But danger always lurked round the corner, and the Popish Plot in 1678 created further alarm and a second wave of persecution in which at least two friars perished. One, John Wall (since canonized) was a member of a Lancashire recusant family who had joined the Franciscan Order at Douai in 1651. In 1656 he came to England and worked for a time in the West country. He was arrested in December 1678 and executed some nine months later. Charles Mahoney, an Irishman who was working in Wales, suffered the same fate a few days earlier. But after this things grew more peaceful, and, in the more tolerant atmosphere of the eighteenth century, life for the friars was much more peaceful.

With a flourishing college and novice-house at Douai, the English province attracted a number of scholarly men. Perhaps the most interesting was Christopher Davenport, born at Merton, near Oxford, in 1598. In 1615 he came under the influence of a Roman Catholic priest and went to the English College in Douai. Here he discovered the Franciscans and was soon afterwards professed as a friar, taking the name of Francis a Sancta Clara. After lecturing there for some years he came back to England and lived, apparently quite peacefully, at Somerset House. Davenport's greatest ambition was to reunite the Anglican and Roman Churches, and he used all his power and contacts for this end. Like Newman, two centuries later, he wrote an exposition of the Thirty-nine Articles trying to prove that they are not as incompatible with Catholic doctrine as many supposed. Later he wrote a book on Catholic principles, a copy of which he presented to Oliver Cromwell, hoping that it might make him more tolerant. Davenport managed to keep out of trouble and lived on until 1680. He was described as 'a Divine of reconciling temper and more disposed to make up breaches than to widen 'em'. He certainly worked hard to bring Anglicans and Roman Catholics to understand and appreciate one another, and, as such, he must be honoured as a herald of the ecumenical movement.

Angelus Mason was a friar of Irish origin who took the name of Angelus a San Francisco and became custos of the English province in 1625. He wrote a number of books, including a manual for members of the Third Order. But his greatest work was his history of the English Franciscan martyrs, which he called *Certamen Seraphicum* and which was published at Douai in 1649. This contains a short history of the Franciscans in England followed by biographical essays on some of the martyrs and it ends with a list of 100 English Franciscan writers from 1224 onwards.

Some years later, Anthony Parkinson, an active friar who was elected Provincial Minister in 1713, wrote a full history of the English Franciscans which he called *Collectanea Anglo-Minoritica*. This is a serious historical book, based on the known authorities, most of which he had discovered in the library of the antiquary, Charles Eyston, at East Hendred in Berkshire. Parkinson, in his preface, is a little apologetic, knowing what most Englishmen thought of papists. He says that if he had chosen to write about the Druids or the old Rhyming Bards people would have been immediately interested to know what he had discovered. This, he says, gives the writer hopes that 'he may not be blamed for rescuing the Characters of many renowned *English Franciscans* from Moths and Worms'. 'They were,' he goes on; 'a society of well-meaning Christians, and our Country-Men; and on these Considerations, I presume, they cannot be disagreable to all'.

In the days when the English Franciscans were still established in England, though becoming slightly moribund, a new branch of the Franciscan family had sprung into being known as the Capuchins. This came about through a group of friars in Italy wanting to live a much stricter form of life, and getting permission, in 1528, to separate from the Order of Friars Minor and live according to their principles. The new Order grew fairly rapidly, spreading northwards and westwards into France, Switzerland, Germany and Spain. In 1597 there was, among the Capuchin novices at Saint Honoré in Paris, an Englishman called William Fitch of Canfield in Essex, generally known as Benedict Canfield. During the next few years, Canfield became an authority on the spiritual life and wrote a book called *The Rule of Perfection* which was published in at least three languages and was widely read throughout the seventeenth century. He also came back as the first Capuchin missionary to these shores, though he was quickly cast into prison and had to return to France on his release in 1601. A few years later, in 1608, an Irish Capuchin, called Francis Nugent, tried to organise a mission to England, Ireland and Scotland, but the Capuchin authorities were slightly suspicious of his methods and gave him little support. Nugent, however, was determined to go ahead with his plans, and a handful of friars came to England in due course. One of them, Angelus Pamel, was imprisoned in 1618, and on his release in 1625 was expelled from the country. In this year, however, some French Capuchins came over in the retinue of Henrietta Maria and were given accommodation at Somerset House, but the Order never made very much progress. During the Civil War some of the friars were put in prison, while others were shipped off to Barbados.

But a few managed to exercise some sort of ministry, saying Mass and giving the sacraments to Roman Catholics in their homes. Their work also took them into hospitals and prisons where they bribed the authorities to let them in. Others moved around furtively, at night and in lay attire, giving help wherever they could. One wrote to say that, during his nine years in England, he had managed to say Mass every day, mostly in private houses but occasionally in the Tower of London or some other prison. The courage and determination of the friars was thus very great, and no doubt there were many women who would like to have shared the dangers and privations with them; but this could not be. A number of English women, however, made their way to France and Belgium and a house of Poor Clares was set up, about 1607, at Gravelines. This became a flourishing community which ran a school for English girls whose parents wished them to be educated in Catholic surroundings. Things went so well that, in 1619, a second house was founded at Aire, and, in 1625, another at Dunkirk. By 1654 there were no less than sixty nuns at Gravelines.

Parallel with this was the establishment of a house of sisters of the Third Order Regular. This was done in 1619 by two English gentlewomen who received the habit in Brussels hoping to be able to set up a convent in England. This however was not possible; so they opened their doors to English ladies who came out to join them. The community soon outgrew its modest accommodation and had to move to Nieuport in 1637 and eventually to Bruges in 1663 where they were given an old palace in which the enclosed community lived for over 100 years.

Towards the end of the seventeenth century the English Friars Minor—known as 'Friars of the Strict Observance' or sometimes as 'Recollects'—found that they could come out of their hiding-places and play a more active and acceptable part in the life of the country. They had already attempted to establish a house in Lincoln's Inn Fields in London, but had had to face some opposition. In 1687 they managed to form a settlement in Birmingham, though this also was destroyed by the mob. But shortly after this they were provided with a house at Osmotherley in Yorkshire where they started a school for young gentlemen. They also ran a school of classics at Putney where boys were educated, mainly in the hope that some of them would enter the priesthood later on. In 1758 there were eleven friars working in London, nine of them holding livings under lay patrons such as the Portuguese and Bavarian embassies.

All of this was, of course, still organised as a mission from the house at Douai which remained the administrative centre of the English province for many years. But at the time of the French Revolution and the dissolution of the religious houses the friars at Douai were told that they must leave. There were then eight priests, one deacon, two novices and seven lay-brothers in the house, and 24 friars working in England. To them the loss of the base at Douai was disastrous. With no seminary, no novice-house, no centre for administration, the English mission began rapidly to deteriorate and the number of friars declined. An attempt was made in 1818 to open a house for the training of novices at Aston and two novices were sent there in 1823. But it was soon found impossible to run a training-centre with so few students; and, in future, English novices were sent to Palestrina instead. In addition to declining numbers there was increasing dissention among the friars which led to a further falling off of postulants. In 1832 Propaganda in Rome was asked to pull things together, but failed to do so; and when the friars met for their Chapter at Clifton in 1838 there were only nine of them left, a tiny group of dispirited men with no corporate life and little heart for their work. Two years later the English province virtually came to an end. It was never officially closed down or suppressed, but it had reached a point where it could no longer function.

The Poor Clares at Gravelines suffered during the French Revolution in the same way that the friars had suffered at Douai. In 1791 the sisters were ordered to abandon their habits and wear lay clothes, so they cut up the curtains in the dormitory to make dresses. Four years later they were told that they must leave the country, and they all returned to England where they settled first at Haggerstone Castle in Yorkshire, then at Scorton and finally near Darlington where they remain to this day.

The same fate befel the Third Order Regular sisters in Bruges. They were dismissed in 1794 and escaped to Holland where they lived for some time in a converted barn near Delft. But this was not a very satisfactory arrangement, so they also came back to England where they were provided with accommodation at Winchester. Then in 1807 they moved to Taunton where they remained for many years.

It was, in fact, from the Tertiary house at Taunton that the friars eventually succeeded in reopening their work. In 1849 a Belgian friar called Bernard van Loo came to England, on the invitation of the Taunton sisters, to see what could be done about restoring the province. At Taunton he met four of the friars left over from the previous foundation, but there was obviously not enough strength in the movement to enable it to restart. A more successful attempt was made in 1858 when three Flemish friars were asked if they would take charge of the Roman Catholic parish of Sclerder in Cornwall. This they did, the only available house being adapted by the younger Pugin to serve the needs of the friars; but again, misfortune overtook them and the place closed down in 1864.

By this time, however, a move had been made to Lancashire where the Catholic population was much larger than in the south-west of England. In 1861 the Bishop of Salford decided that the new parish of West Gorton in Manchester should be run by Franciscan friars, and a group of four, led by a Belgian called Emmanuel Kenners, duly arrived. At first, like the friars in the thirteenth century, they lived in a cottage, but, as the community grew, a friary was eventually built. From that time onwards more and more parishes were entrusted to the friars—in London, at Forest Gate, and so on. There are now 19 houses of Friars Minor in Great Britain including a House of Studies at Canterbury which replaced the house at East Bergholt in 1973. The English Province is also responsible for missionary work in India, South Africa and Peru.

At the time when the Observants were trying to restart their province in England, the Capuchins were also anxious to restore their mission which had been closed for some time. The first Capuchin to arrive in England was an Italian friar called Luigi di Lavagna. Luigi had worked for a time in France and had been invited to go to Canada by the Bishop of Toronto. With this in mind he came to England to learn the language, and acted as chaplain to a sisterhood in Peckham. While there Luigi felt so strongly the need for a Capuchin mission to England that he gave up all idea of going to Canada and returned to the continent in search of recruits. The first to join him was a Belgian called Seraphin of Bruges, who did not stay long, and the next an Austrian called Lawrence of Imst.

Hearing of the good work which these two Capuchin friars were doing for the Catholic population in London, Viscount Feilding, a recent convert, felt that he would like to help them. He was, at the time of his conversion, building a church for the Anglicans on his estate in North Wales. He now decided to give the church, when completed, to the Capuchins—much to the sorrow and indignation of some of the villagers. This was at Pantasaph to which the little band of friars moved in 1852. There were now four of them, but all foreigners, and they were shortly joined by Seraphin of Bruges who became their superior. As well as looking after the Catholics in the neighbourhood, the friars conducted missions first in Wales and then in England, as a result of which other houses were founded—in London, Chester, Crawley and elsewhere. But Pantasaph was, and is still, the mother house of the Capuchin Order in England.

In 1867 the English Capuchin houses were formed into a custody of the province of the Netherlands, but in 1873 the friars were thought to be sufficiently settled to create an English province which was dedicated to St. Lawrence of Brindisi. Then, early in the twentieth century, the friars established a house in Oxford where students could stay while working at the University. This, for a time, was called Grosseteste House to commemorate the good work done for the friars by Robert Grosseteste in the thirteenth century. It was here that the most distinguished of English Capuchins did much of his work, Father Cuthbert. Cuthbert of Brighton, as he was officially called, had gone to the Capuchins at Pantasaph in 1881 at the age of 15 to test his vocation. He was, in due course, professed and worked for a time in Crawley and in London. He soon began to show an interest in history, and while working in London he founded a society for the study of the Franciscan sources which he called 'Twentieth-century Franciscans'. This was in 1905 when the study of early Franciscan literature was at its height and just before the foundation of the British Society for Franciscan Studies which published its first volume in 1908. Then in 1910 Fr. Cuthbert moved to Oxford where he acted as superior of Grosseteste House for many years during which he wrote his *Life of St. Francis* (1912) and his *History of the Capuchins* (1929) both of which are still standard works. He was also of a deeply pastoral spirit and in 1905 visited the hop-pickers in Kent and worked among them for some weeks, thus inaugurating a scheme which was later taken up by members of other Churches.

The Capuchins have always seen their role as missionaries, and they have worked hard to bring home to people the message of the Gospel and the need for prayer and sacrament. In order to provide literature for those whom they were trying to help they launched, in 1877, a monthly magazine called *Franciscan Annals* which contained a good deal of devotional and historical material, Franciscan news, short stories, poems and so on. This magazine and those published by the Friars Minor—*The Franciscan Herald* (1887) and *Franciscan Monthly* (1897) have been greatly valued by the increasing number of tertiaries.

The last to arrive on the English scene were the Conventuals. In 1905 Fr. Bonaventure Scerberras of Malta came to England on a preaching mission. In the following year he returned with the idea of setting up a house of his Order in England, and in 1907 he was put in charge of a small parish at Portishead near Bristol where he was joined by two Americans and a German. In 1910 he managed to found a second house in Rye, but it was some time before any Englishmen felt inclined to join them. This prompted them to move north, and, before long they managed to acquire two houses, one in Liverpool and the other in Manchester. By 1955 there were six houses and about 40 friars—enough to allow them to become a separate province, having previously been dependent on the province of the Immaculate Conception in America. There are now twelve centres in England, one of them at Canterbury where the friars help in running the Franciscan Study Centre attached to the University of Kent.

In 1850 there was, at the house of Colettine Poor Clares in Bruges, a saintly abbess called Mary Domenic Berlamonte who ruled the house for forty years during which she was responsible for founding fourteen new convents, four of them in England. In this year a descendent of the family who had sheltered the Minoresses at the time of the dissolution provided accommodation for a house of Poor Clares at Baddesley-Clinton in Warwickshire to which Mother Mary came, bringing with her six choir-nuns and three extern sisters. In 1857 a house was founded in Notting Hill, another at Manchester in 1868, after which others sprang up in different parts of the country. There are also a good many houses of enclosed members of the Third Order though most of them are independent, such as the Franciscan Sisters of Mary, the Franciscan Sisters of Mill Hill, the Franciscan Minoresses, and others. Of unenclosed tertiaries there is a very large company who are proud to be associated with the Order of St. Francis.

The Franciscan movement in England for the past hundred years or so has thus been mainly a pastoral and missionary form of ministry. Among the friars the Rule which St. Francis drew up in 1223 is kept as strictly as is possible bearing in mind the very different conditions in which men must live today and also the needs and demands of their ministry. Life is simple, disciplined and devout, as St. Francis would have wished it to be; and if the modern friar avoids the more spectacular forms of service and self-sacrifice, there are a great many people who, as tertiaries, parishioners or friends, have heard through their ministry, the voice of St. Francis speaking to them and exhorting them to simplicity, humility, care and concern for others, and, above all, devotion to Christ and his Church.

10

ANGLICAN FRANCISCANS

In the middle of the nineteenth century, when the Observant and Capuchin friars were once more getting established in England, members of the Church of England were not generally greatly interested in St. Francis whom they found something of an enigma. Henry Hallam, in his *View of the State of Europe in the Middle Ages*, which was a popular and widely-read book, described St. Francis as 'a harmless enthusuast, pious and sincere, but hardly of sound mind'. Henry Milman, Dean of St. Paul's, in his *History of Latin Christianity* (1855) wrote: 'St. Francis was endowed with that fervour of mystic devotion which spread like an epidemic among the lower orders throughout Christendom. It was a superstition, but a superstition which had such an earnestness, warmth, tenderness, as to raise the religious feeling to an intense but gentle passion'. But a few years later, in 1868, Mrs. Oliphant wrote a sympathetic life of St. Francis; and from then onwards, Anglicans took an interest in him, reading English translations of the early sources and of the popular life by Léopold de Chérancé (1879).

Study of the Franciscans in England in the Middle Ages was now beginning to receive some interest. In 1858 the Rev. J.S. Brewer edited a volume called *Monumenta Franciscana* to which he contributed a preface of over 100 pages. Thirty years later a Norfolk clergyman, called Augustus Jessopp, wrote an essay on the first English Franciscans which he published in a book called *The Coming of the Friars*. Then, in 1892, A. G. Little, then aged 29, published his historical account of the Grey

Friars in Oxford which set the standard for all future work on Franciscan history. Two years later an English translation of Sabatier's *Vie de Saint François* was published, and the floodgates were opened for a deluge of books about the saint which continues right down to the present day.

By the year 1900 interest in St. Francis and the Franciscan movement was spreading rapidly, partly in the field of historical research and partly in general interest and admiration. St. Francis certainly appealed very much to a public which was becoming more and more concerned about the sufferings and privations of the poor, which was fascinated by all that was medieval and romantic, and which was yearning for a more simple life without the luxuries and extravagances which so many people sought after. Those who were thinking along one or more of these lines found St. Francis a fascinating and wholly admirable character. He was obviously a very 'human' saint, a man who lived among lepers, who talked so simply about God, who loved animals so much that he would pick up worms to prevent them being trodden on, and who would invite all creation to join with him in singing the praises of the Creator. Out of all this interest and enthusiasm three things emerged—a flood of popular literature about St. Francis and the friars, a thorough investigation of Franciscan history, and a desire to found, in the Church of England, something similar to the Order of Friars Minor as it had been in the days of St. Francis himself.

The man who really started the active, professed, Anglican Franciscan movement was a priest called James Adderley who, in 1893, became vicar of Plaistow in East London which was then a very poor district. Adderley was inspired by the story of St. Francis and his companions to want to start there a community of men who would take certain simple vows and devote themselves to the service of the poor. He had already enlisted the help of a priest called Chappel, and, in 1894, he persuaded a young man called Ernest Hardy (later known as Brother Andrew) to join him. These three men decided to follow, as far as possible, the principles laid down by St. Francis. They were to live a life of austerity and poverty while they did their utmost to bring both spiritual and material help to their neighbours. They called their brotherhood 'The Society of the Divine Compassion' which they described as 'a community of priests, deacons and communicant laymen, banded together in a common life of poverty, chastity and obedience for the glory of our Lord and Saviour Jesus Christ and for the benefit of His Holy Catholic Church: to worship Him and to work for Him in all mankind, especially the poor and suffering, in imitation of the Divine Master, seeking the help of one another in thus obeying Him'. Although this does not mention St. Francis, the Society intended to be a modern Franciscan movement and its members wore the brown habit and the knotted cord.

The life which they lived was one of discipline, simplicity and service. They gave hospitality, so far as they could, to any in need, sometimes giving up their beds to homeless and destitute men and sleeping on the floor. They ministered to the patients in an isolation hospital during the small-pox epidemic of 1901−2. They opened, at East Hanningfield, the Homes of St. Giles where they looked after lepers who, at that time, were not admitted to the existing hospitals. They were prepared to go anywhere and do anything. The calls on their slender resources were so great that they themselves were sometimes reduced to a diet of dry bread and tea.

The little brotherhood never became very large; but,

in 1902, it was joined by William Stirr, now aged forty, who had also been moved by the Franciscan ideal and, when a curate in Vauxhall, had lived in a common lodging-house in order to identify himself with the poor. Fr. William had in him much of the mysticism which one associates with some of the early friars, and he eventually found his vocation, not in a community, but as a solitary. As there was no enclosed community for men in the Church of England, William went to live in some old stables at Glasshampton in Worcestershire where he lived the life of a hermit. He always hoped that others might join him in his austere and silent life; but none came, and William remained there alone for eighteen years.

While all this was going on, the Franciscan inspiration had caught hold of an enthusiastic young priest in Peckham called George Potter. In 1923 he turned his parsonage—which was not a vicarage but a derelict public-house—into a home for a small community of friars and for homeless and destitute boys. The members of the fellowship, who called themselves the Brotherhood of the Holy Cross, wore the Franciscan habit and had a simple rule, but this had to be flexible if it was not to interfere with their parochial and rescue work.

Both of these experiments were attempts to adapt the Franciscan way of life to a parochial ministry. Members of both communities saw their work as ministry to the poor, the homeless, the lepers. In order to do this they took vows of poverty, chastity and obedience, and tried to organise their life on a simple rule of prayer, service and self-sacrifice. One thing they did not do was to 'identify' themselves with the poor and the destitute. However poor they were in their way of living, they always had a home to go to. But St. Francis would not allow his friars to have even this.

So the next attempt to introduce a Franciscan way of life was more drastic and more demanding. This was to live among the most poverty-stricken and destitute of all people—the tramps, the homeless—and to live as they lived. The priest who felt called to this way of life was a man called Brother Giles. In the 1920s there were, in England, a great many tramps who slept rough, or in the Casual Wards of the workhouses, and who had nothing that they could call their own except the rags in which they stood and a small bundle of bits and pieces that they carried about with them. It was to these men that Brother Giles went as a Christian missioner. Hungry, dirty, cold, verminous and wet, he tramped with the tramps and slept huddled up with them in what were often filthy conditions. He made friends with men who had no other friend in the world. He told them about Christ and his love for all men. He endured every kind of privation in order to carry out his vocation in the spirit of St. Francis.

After some years of this life, Brother Giles began to feel the strain, and his friends insisted upon his being provided with a house to which he could somtimes go for rest and refreshment. The place chosen was a farmhouse in Dorset which had recently been the scene of an experiment in the rehabilitation of young delinquents, run by an American called Homer Lane and known as The Little Commonwealth. Giles, and any others who were drawn to his form of ministry, made this their base for a year or two; but, before long, his health broke up and he had to go.

The Committee of well-wishers were very anxious that the mission should be continued, and invited the Chaplain of Worcester College, Oxford, Douglas Downes, to come and take on the house and try to build up a community which would preserve something of the devotion and dedication of Brother Giles. Downes, who was thenceforth known as 'Brother Douglas', went to the Farm in 1922 as a stop-gap and remained there, or was connected with it, for the rest of his life.

Flowers Farm at Cerne Abbas was really three things. It was a religious community, a small group of men who lived a disciplined life, saying the customary offices and having time for prayer and meditation. At first they wore the clothes of working men, but before long they adopted the Franciscan habit which they wore wherever they went. Secondly, it was a refuge for the homeless, some of whom stayed only a single night while others were allowed to remain there for many years. The main object of the Community was to pick out, from among the tramps, young men who could be trained as gardeners and house-boys and for whom good jobs could eventually be found. Thirdly, it was a base from which missions could go out to the men on the roads. Every so often one or two of the friars would go off for a fortnight among the tramps, sleeping in Casual Wards and common lodging-houses, making friends with their companions and trying to bring some hope into their hard and sordid lives.

Brother Douglas' approach to his work was essentially practical. He felt deeply for the men, especially the young men, caught in the trap of vagrancy, and longed to do something to set them free. He would go to them, or he would try to get them to come to him. He wanted more and more homes where men could find peace and hope. He helped to found a society called the Vagrancy Reform Society, and he went about preaching sermons and making speeches about the scandal of the men and women on the roads. Twice he appeared before a group of prominent members of Parliament in London, gave them some first-hand information of the state of the Casual Wards, and pleaded with them to see that the conditions were improved.

Douglas' energy and enthusiasm led to the setting up of homes in Cornwall, Sussex, Hertfordshire, Wales, Scotland and elsewhere. His ideal was a hostel in every town and a home in every county; but this was asking too much. Even if money were forthcoming they would need dedicated men to run the homes and hostels, and these were hard to find. For in spite of all his attractiveness and charm, and his obvious holiness of life and depth of faith, Brother Douglas failed to draw men into the brotherhood, and the number of friars never got above four or five. Men did not seem to want to live this kind of life. This may have been due to the fact that there was not enough discipline and tranquility for a religious community. Prayers were said and a simple pattern of life was observed, but there was no novitiate and no proper rule. The practical side of their life—work, looking after their visitors, tramping the roads—took up too much time. Brother Douglas was the sort of man who prays while he works, but not everyone can do this. If, therefore, the work was to expand men must be attracted to the community.

It was in 1934, after they had been going for twelve years, that the friars had their first Retreat, and it was conducted by Fr. Algy Robertson, the vicar of St. Ives near Huntingdon. Fr. Algy had worked in India, where he had been a member of the Christa Seva Sangha, a brotherhood who adopted an Indian way of life and associated with the poorer elements in society. When he came back to England he brought some of his friends with him and organised a small religious community in his vicarage, run on Franciscan lines. He was naturally interested in other communities of this kind—the Brotherhood of St. Francis, the Society of the Divine Compassion, the Brotherhood of the Holy Cross and others—and tried to draw them together into a common enterprise. Among other plans he proposed that aspirants to all these brotherhoods should be trained together as novices. He thought Cerne Abbas the only place where this could be done, and in the end, he decided to leave St. Ives and settle at the friary in Dorset. He soon became the obvious leader of the movement, giving the place a more monastic look, tightening up discipline, and turning a loosely-knit brotherhood into a religious order. At this point the old Brotherhood of St. Francis disappeared, and its place was taken by the Society of St. Francis. Brother Douglas, while remaining titular head of the Society went off to do other things—in England, Germany, Canada and elsewhere—still concerned with the needs of the poorest members of society, still sharing their lives with them.

Meanwhile, under new management, the Society began to grow rapidly as young men found in it what they were looking for. With increased numbers new forms of work were planned—a school at Hooke for maladjusted boys, a house at Cambridge where students could learn about the Society and its aims, several parishes which the friars served in various places, a hostel in Stepney for coloured men. The Society at Cerne Abbas had close links with the friars working in Plaistow and in Peckham, and they took over Fr. William's little monastery at Glasshampton and made it the place to which novices were sent for training. Later they acquired a house at Alnmouth in Northumberland to serve as a base for their work in the north of England and Scotland. Finally, in the midst

118

of the recent troubles, they established a small community in Belfast. Meanwhile bishops overseas began to realise what good work they were doing and asked for friars to be sent to help them in their work. In 1959 a friar went out to New Guinea, and, in the next few years, communities were set up in Zambia and Tanzania, in Australia and in the United States. The little community of four men presided over by Brother Douglas in 1935 has now become a Society of 122 professed friars and 56 novices, divided into four provinces and 24 separate houses in five continents.

The Society of St. Francis is obviously different from the old Brotherhood at Flowers Farm. There are now no road-missions, but a lot of rehabilitation work in the communities where the friars try to help alcoholics, drug-addicts, ex-prisoners, and all those who fail in some way or other to come to terms with life. Life is still extremely simple with regular prayer and a lot of practical work. Many of the friars take part in parochial missions. Visits are paid to schools, prisons, and hospitals. Poverty is still the ideal, and the friars have a rule that any money which they may have in hand at the end of each half-year shall be given away.

It is natural that some women, like St Clare, should wish to be associated with the friars in their life of poverty and service, but only a few houses have been established —the Community of St. Clare at Freeland, near Oxford, which lives a contemplative and enclosed life as did the sisters at San Damiano many centuries ago, and an older house, the Community of St. Francis at South Petherton in Somerset, an active community founded in 1905 for nursing and mission-work, which has become affiliated to the friars. The Franciscan Servants of Jesus and Mary at Crediton was founded in 1930 and was at one time interested in the idea of joining the other Franciscan groups in 1934, but has remained independent. Meanwhile a vigorous Third Order has grown up for people who wish to be associated with the work of the friars, and who are prepared to adhere to a rule of life based on the Franciscan principles of simplicity, self-sacrifice and prayer. There is, thus, a flourishing Franciscan movement in the Church of England and in the Anglican Communion throughout the world.

The year 1974 marks the 750th anniversary of the arrival in England of the first Franciscans. During those seven and a half centuries much has happened and big changes have taken place, especially with the great upheaval of the sixteenth century, the separation of the Church in England from the Apostolic See, and the dissolution of all the religious houses. There have, during these centuries, been times when it seemed likely that the Franciscan flame would be put out; but there have always been revivals and renewals as the inspiration of St. Francis has touched the hearts and minds of men and women and urged them to make great sacrifices in order to obey the divine purposes as interpreted by St. Francis himself.

Francis had no other wish than to be faithful in carrying out what Christ had told his disciples to do. He had been prepared to risk all in total obedience to the divine will, and he expected those who joined him to be equally bold and reckless in their self-giving.

The story of the Franciscans in England shows that, although there have been times of progress and times of stagnation, the high standards laid down by St. Francis have stood firm. The poverty of the first friars, the courage of those who preferred to give their lives rather than to surrender their faith, the endurance and patience of those who faced the horors and indignities of the Casual Ward—all this shows how strong is the influence of the Little Poor Man of Assisi who, at the end of his life of hardship and suffering said to his friends:

'I have done my duty; may Christ teach you yours.'

A NOTE ON BOOKS

The chief source for the early history of the Franciscans in England is the *Chronicle of Thomas of Eccleston*, of which there are several translations. The latest is by Leo Serley-Price, and is called *The Coming of the Franciscans* (1964).

For background history, the standard work on the friars in the Middle Ages is John R. H. Moorman, *A History of the Franciscan Order* (1968). For the history of the friars in England see:

A. G. Little, *Studies in English Franciscan History* (1917)
Edward Hutton, *The Franciscans in England* (1926)
V. G. Green, *The Franciscans in Medieval English Life* (1939)

There are full-length histories of the friars in Oxford (by A. G. Little), in Cambridge (by J. R. H. Moorman), in London (by C. L. Kingsford) and in Canterbury (by C. Cotton). Anthony Parkinson's *Collectanea Anglo-Minoritica* (1726) contains a great deal of useful information.

For post-Reformation history, see Fr. Thaddeus, *The Franciscans in England, 1600–1850* (1898). J. M. Stone's *Faithful Unto Death* (1892) should be read with caution.

For the Capuchins, the standard work is Fr. Cuthbert, *The Capuchins*, 2 vols. (1928). See also Fr. Sebastian, *The Capuchins* (1963). For the Conventuals see John Jukes, *English Province of the Order of Friars Minor Conventual* (1967).

The history of the Poor Clares in the Middle Ages will be found in A. F. C. Bourdillon, *The Order of Minoresses in England* (1926). For later history see Anon. *St. Clare and her Order* (1912).

For the history of the Anglican Franciscans, see:

K. E. Burne, *The Life and Letters of Father Andrew* (1948)
G. Curtis, *William of Glasshampton* (1947).
Fr. Francis, *Brother Douglas* (1959).
Fr. Denis, *Father Algy* (1964).